broth & stock
from the Nourished Kitchen

broth
& stock

from the **Nourished Kitchen**

wholesome master recipes for
bone, vegetable, and seafood broths
and meals to make with them

Jennifer McGruther

TEN SPEED PRESS
Berkeley

contents

chapter 3
poultry

chapter 4
meat

chapter 5
fish

chapter 6
vegetables

introduction

Most days of the week, I keep an enameled cast-iron pot on the back burner of my stove where bones simmer in water to make broth. I sip this broth in the morning sprinkled with sea salt, chopped fresh garlic, and flat-leaf parsley. I add it to soups and stews, gravies and sauces, and it is perpetually present at the kitchen table in some form or another. Broth nourishes the body and soothes the soul. I remember how a mug of golden, rich chicken broth or a bowl of chicken soup laced with noodles and dotted with carrots and celery seemed to alleviate childhood colds, or how beef vegetable soup fortified my sister and me against a cold winter day. Few foods offer such resolute and heartening comfort.

Broth always seems to appear in little bursts of my memory. There was the rich matzo ball soup my grandfather and I shared ritualistically during my visits to New York as a child. There was my first taste of dashi, a Japanese broth made from seaweed and bonito flakes, when I moved with my family from the United States to Japan at six. And there were the steadfast red-and-white cans full of beef and barley or tomato soup that lurked in my cupboard growing up.

Broths and stocks, soups, stews, and sauces find a well-loved and much deserved place in kitchens throughout the world. While they form the foundation of professional cooking, broths and stocks, at their heart, are foods for the home. They are foods not only of comfort, but also of frugality and the pressure to waste as little as possible, lest bellies go hungry. In this way, to make broth not only fills the functional role of sating hunger and thirst, but also teaches us a lesson in the values of patience, simplicity, and thrift. There is virtue in the humble soup pot.

patience

Making broth is an experience of delayed gratification. In an age where nearly everything is immediately available with the tap of a finger on a screen, the development and pursuit of patience is a virtue that needs exercising. To extract the goodness of broth, its flavor, gelatin-rich protein, and trace minerals, depends upon several patient hours of simmering. Broth is not the stuff of quick and easy thirty-minute meals, so plan accordingly. You don't need to tend your stockpot with ever-vigilant care, but it does take many hours for bones to release their nutrients and for bony cuts of meat to surrender their flavor before falling apart into beautiful tenderness. After all, good food takes good time.

simplicity

With few exceptions, making broths and stocks is wonderfully simple. If you can boil water, you can make a good broth. The simplest of stocks require nothing more than bones, water, and a pot to cook them in. Among the best broths, stocks and bone broths, (both commercially prepared and homemade) that we tested for the Nourished Kitchen website were not those with the most herbs and spices or aromatic vegetables added to the pot; rather, the stocks and broths our taste testers favored the most were those that contained the least—nothing more than bones and water, with a sprinkling of sea salt for good measure. This produces a pure, neutrally flavored liquid that is lovely on its own as well as adaptable to suit the needs of the individual dishes you make from it.

thrift

Inexpensive to make, broths and stocks are powerfully nutritious but cost-effective food. You can purchase bones straight from ranchers, farmers, and butchers for a fraction of the cost of prime cuts of meat, while the spent frames of roasted chickens and turkeys coupled with vegetable scraps make a broth that costs little to cook at home. In saving what you can, you minimize food waste in your home and eke out every bit of nutrition from the foods you offer your family.

broth and history

Bone broths feature prominently in traditional food pathways around the world. When food is scarce, no one can afford the luxury of waste. Native Americans prepared bone broths first by lining baskets with clay so that they could hold water, arranging the bones of wild game inside them, and pouring in water. They would drop stones heated in campfires into the baskets, which would then heat the water to make broth. Chicken and fish broths feature prominently in the traditional cooking of Asia, and long-simmered broths made from beef marrow form the base of several traditional Korean dishes.

While bones need to simmer for several hours to several days before they will release their nutrients and flavor, broths and stocks are in many ways the original fast food. In medieval times, innkeepers kept a pot of soup, sometimes called the hunter's pot, hanging over the hearth, from which they could readily feed passersby. Never fully emptied, the pot hung perpetually at the ready, with innkeepers replacing its contents as needed, adding more meaty bones, starchy roots, herbs, ale, and stale bread throughout the week, so that a warming, satisfying potage lay waiting, ready to welcome travelers. All one needed to do was ladle it into a bowl.

Long-simmered broths also serve as the inspiration for one of the first restaurants in Europe. The word *restaurant* comes from the French word *restorer*, meaning, as you might guess, "to restore." A man by the name of Boulanger opened the first restuarant in Paris in the eighteenth century, serving only broths and soups. His sign, the legend goes, read VENITE AD ME VOS QUI STOMACHO LABORATIS ET EGO RESTAURABO VOS, or, "Come to me, all who labor in the stomach, and I will restore you." From that sign, his shop became known as a restaurant. And soon any place dedicated to preparing meals on site and serving them to paying diners became known as a restaurant, too. It all started with good broth.

While restaurants began to flourish and inns continued to sate travelers' hunger with hearty potage, stews, broths, and soups, home cooks began making portable soup (page 93)—hard, glassy nuggets made from reducing broth and then drying it further. This process, which preserved the broth by removing as much of its liquid as possible, created one of the first convenience foods, ready for travel. Having made portable soup, travelers would still be able to fill their bellies with good nourishment when ready

access to food was not a guarantee. On their journey westward, the explorers Lewis and Clark carried with them nearly two hundred pounds of portable soup, which nourished them and their companions throughout their travels and which they also used for trade.

The nineteenth century's industrial revolution made manufacturing easier, and it also created an opportunity for enterprising businessmen to begin producing convenience foods. Previously, making portable soup had been a laborious process that took home cooks enormous amounts of time to prepare from scratch. They began by cutting enormous bones into smaller pieces that fit into their cooking vessels. Then came the process of simmering the bones to make broth, degreasing the stock, reducing it until it formed a viscous, gelatinous liquid, and finally drying it out to form small nuggets or brittle slabs. Industrial manufacturing changed all that. It alleviated the burden of preparing portable soup at home, by producing it quickly and easily, in vast quantities. By the early part of the twentieth century, with the isolation of the amino acid glutamine and eventual manufacturing of monosodium glutamate (better known as MSG), powdery bouillon cubes replaced gelatin-rich portable soup. Consumers seeking ease and convenience in the kitchen began to replace the process of making stock and broth in the home by purchasing bouillon cubes to flavor soups, stews, gravies, and sauces.

glutamate, bouillon, and broth

A nineteenth-century German chemist first identified glutamic acid after treating wheat gluten, for which he named it, with sulfuric acid in 1866. Forty years later, a Japanese scientist working out of Tokyo Imperial University isolated glutamic acid from kombu, a seaweed that gives the traditional Japanese broth, dashi, (page 39) its unique, elusive savory flavor that is not sweet, salty, bitter, or sour. He described this flavor as "umami" and later isolated its chemical constituents and patented them as monosodium glutamate (MSG), which then became widely available as seasoning for both commercial and home kitchens, marketed as Accent.

Processed-food manufacturers often—though not always—add MSG to bouillon cubes and broth bases as a way to enhance their flavor, attempting to re-create those elusive, savory umami notes found in homemade broth. Broth tends to be high in naturally occurring glutamic acid. Some people are sensitive to MSG and might express sensitivity to the naturally occurring glutamate found in broths and stocks.

Like many amino acids, glutamic acid performs many functions and plays an important role in cognitive function as well as digestive health. Recent research into gut health and amino acids indicates that glutamine helps mitigate gut permeability and also enhances the mucosal structure of the gut, which may be one reason why bone broths are traditionally heralded as easy-to-digest foods for those recovering from illness. In studies on mice, researchers found that supplementation with glutamine helped reduce markers of inflammation.

gelatin in broth

If you've ever roasted a chicken or turkey and left it on the counter or in the fridge overnight only to find that its juices congealed, you've made gelatin. Bones, skin, joints, and connective tissue are naturally rich in collagen. When you drop collagen-rich cuts of meat and bone into your pot, cover them with liquid like water, and turn up the heat, that collagen transforms into gelatin. Gelatin is what gives broth its silky-smooth texture when hot and its characteristic bouncy gelled texture when it cools. Gelatin is rich in protein, and while it is not a complete protein in and of itself, it acts as a protein sparer, helping the protein you do eat go a little further. The proteins that form gelatin, glycine and proline, have anti-inflammatory properties, and some evidence indicates they may help reduce signs of aging.

using broths, bone broths, and stocks

Ever-present in the culinary traditions of peoples around the world, broth provides the foundation for many traditional foods, including soups, stews, sauces, and aspics. You can keep master broths and stocks, like those included within this book, on hand and use them to prepare wholesome meals from scratch.

In preparing homemade broths, you participate in the tradition of kitchen wisdom that has nourished the bodies and satisfied the bellies of generations upon generations of healthy people worldwide. It's a simple, but a powerful practice.

the broth maker's kitchen

Broth and stock form the foundation of my cooking, and I try to keep them on hand in the kitchen so I can use them at a moment's notice. I begin by simmering bones or meat, water, and wine together, sometimes adding herbs, aromatic vegetables, and spices to the pot. Simmered for several hours on my stove top over low heat so that it barely bubbles, it forms a beautiful liquid. I then strain out the richly colored liquid that can range from pale yellow to a deep coffee brown. This protein-dense broth or stock with a trace of minerals finds its way into many of the dishes I make at home, including soups and stews, sauces and gravies, risottos and pilaf, giving each a boost of nourishment and infusing them with a savory yet neutral flavor. It is this same recipe that also finds its way into my mug on a chilly winter morning and into the soup pot with noodles when my little boy feels the sniffles coming on.

what's the difference between broth, stock, and bone broth?

Broths, stocks, and bone broths–primarily built on the same foundation of meat and bone, vegetable and herb, vinegar or wine–bear many similarities. These flavor-forward liquids provide the fundamental basis for many beloved dishes around the world, such as soups and stews, sauces and gravies, and braising liquids for meats or vegetables, and are lovely enjoyed in their own right. When cooking, you can typically exchange one for another easily and without much, if any, conspicuous difference in the outcome of the final dish. While there are subtle and important differences, I generally use the term "broth" as a catch-all in this introductory text.

broth

At its simplest, broth is the liquid that is left after you've simmered or cooked meat. Composed primarily of meat, water, and perhaps some vegetables or herbs thrown in the pot for good measure, broths are quick-cooking by comparison to stocks and bone broths. Thinner in body and lighter in flavor than stocks and bone broths, broths based on meat come together in just a few hours. Their flavor is meat-forward, and they do well as a basis for simple soups or sipped on their own.

In folk medicine, home cooks traditionally fed meat broths to the convalescent, the ill, and the infirm: new mothers recuperating from the rigors of birth, infants just off the breast, the elderly whose teeth couldn't withstand tough foods, as well as those recovering from illness and whose constitution required soft, nutrient-dense, healing foods. When solid foods and full meals prove undesirable, broths provide easy, comforting nourishment. These healing recipes invariably called for boiling meat gently over a hot flame, skimming it to remove any scum that appeared at the surface, and serving it by the cup with a pinch of salt. As the ill family member's health improved, minced well-boiled meat, herbs, and cooked barley, or other grains were added to the pot, and eventually the patient's diet returned to solid food.

stock

Where meat provides the base for broths, bones provide the base for stocks and, in this way, they're nearly indistinguishable from bone broths in a practical, culinary sense. Bones, cartilage, and whatever connective tissue happens to adhere to them are dropped into a pot of water to form the foundation of stock. When simmered for several hours, this combination of bone, cartilage, and connective tissue gives stock the luxurious, silky-smooth texture that meat-based broths lack. Vegetables, herbs, and spices can enliven stocks, much as they do broths, infusing them with the flavors of whatever dish you plan to prepare. While broths are often sipped on their own or speckled with meat, herbs, vegetables, and grains to serve as the base for loose, liquid soups, stocks, by contrast, serve as the foundation for many dishes: a liquid in which to braise meats or vegetables or the foundation for sauces, gravies, hearty soups, and stews.

While meat-based broths typically cook for an hour or two, stocks cook much longer. A good rule of thumb to consider is that chicken and poultry stocks simmer for three to four hours, while stocks made from beef, pork, or lamb bones simmer for six to ten hours, or until the stock is rich in flavor with a silky body.

Cooks further divide stocks by classifying them as either white stocks (made from uncooked bones) or brown stocks (prepared with roasted bones). Roasting bones enriches stocks and bone broths with light caramel and deeply savory notes, while white stocks tend to taste lighter and less complex.

bone broth

Just as with stocks, bones form the foundation of bone broths. So if they're made with the same fundamental ingredients as stock, you might wonder exactly what the difference is.

While stocks simmer for several hours until richly flavored, bone broths cook for considerably longer, often for a half a day or up to two full days. At completion, the bones will have simmered so long that they typically crumble when pinched between the thumb and forefinger. This extended cooking time produces extremely flavorful results and extracts as much gelatin as possible as well as some minerals from the bones and connective tissue. You can use the protein-rich bone broth as you would either broth or stock; that is, as the foundation for soups and stews, to braise meats or vegetables, to stir into pilafs and risottos, for sauces and gravies, or, as many people enjoy it, sipped on its own.

Long-simmered bone broths play a prominent role in culinary traditions worldwide. Not only did preparing bone broths eliminate waste and maximize the use of the whole animal—an appealing idea when food is scarce—but it also provided much-needed nourishment as an excellent source of protein, and offered something safe to drink, as available water was not always clean. Anthropologists have identified deer marrow bone broths as a vital source of nourishment in Native American traditional food pathways.

choosing bones

When making stocks and bone broths, you're after a deep and rich flavor as well as a luxurious, silky texture. The silkiness in a good bone broth comes from the gelatin that forms when the collagen in the cartilage and connective tissue that adheres to bones dissolves into your cooking liquid. When you choose bones for your broth, keep in mind that those that have the most connective tissue and cartilage make the best broth, one that will be smooth in texture and rich in protein.

As animals age, they lose cartilage, so the stocks made from the bones of younger animals typically set to a stronger gel with less time on the stove than the stock made from bones of older animals. Flavor, in both meat and bones, increases as animals age and with the amount of exercise an animal is permitted to undertake, so the bones from older animals typically produce a more strongly flavored broth than that made from younger animals.

While bones with plenty of connective tissue, like knuckles and trotters, give body to bone broths and stocks, neck bones and marrowbones contribute flavor and richness. Partnering them together in the stockpot produces bone broths and stocks with a beautiful gel and silky texture, and a good flavor, too. Always strive for balance when making stocks and bone broths, taking care to add a good mix of marrow-rich, jointed, and meaty bones to your pot.

chicken, turkey, and poultry bones

Bones from chickens, turkeys, and other birds make beautiful broths. If you roast a chicken for Sunday dinner or a turkey for Thanksgiving, save

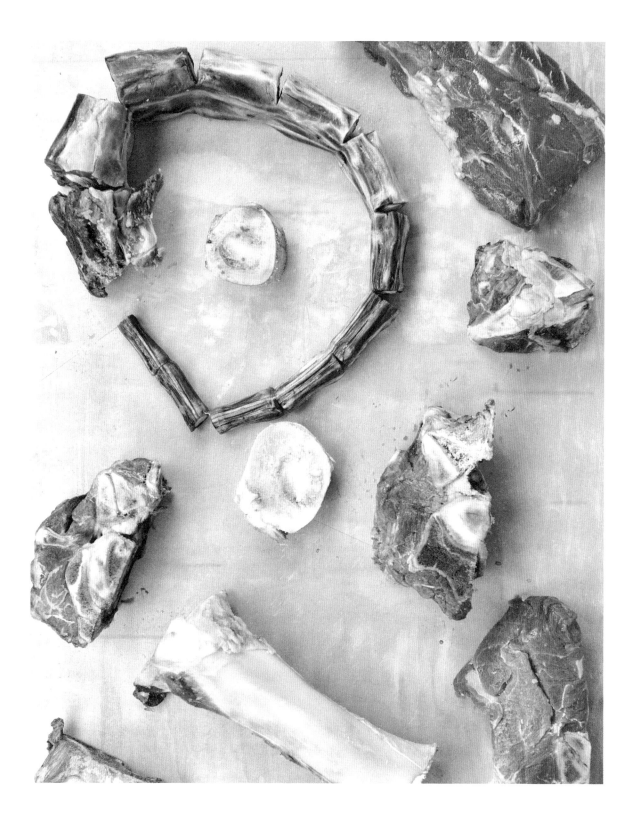

the bird's carcass for the stockpot. This frame already includes meaty bones, marrow-rich bones like the leg bones, and cartilage-rich bones like the breastbone. A few chicken or turkey feet, scrubbed clean, trimmed (see page 31), and thrown into the pot with the rest of the bird's bones, will produce a particularly gelatinous broth. If you can stomach them, chicken heads, plucked and cleaned, also produce a gelatinous broth, as the bird's comb is an excellent source of collagen. Of course, unless you happen to process the birds yourself, you're unlikely to find these parts available for purchase anywhere.

When butchers process birds, cutting away the breasts, thighs, and drumsticks to sell by the piece, the other cuts remain. There's little market for chicken backs and necks, so you can typically pick these up for a very reasonable price. Brown these bones and save them for the stockpot.

beef, veal, lamb, and pork bones

Bones from larger animals, like domestic ruminants and pigs, produce a robust stock or bone broth that stands up well to strong, earthy, and hearty flavors like beets and other root vegetables, as well as tomatoes, beans, and split peas. When making beef, lamb, or pork stock or bone broth, look for a wide variety of bones. Meaty neck bones will give a rich flavor to your bone broths and stocks. Knucklebones and oxtails are a good source of connective tissue, and they will produce a protein-rich gelatin, while marrow bones will flavor your stocks and bone broths and render their fat, which you can scoop off and use to fry potatoes or sauté vegetables.

When I buy pork bones for making bone broth, I aim for a variety of bones, just as I do with beef. I usually select a variety of neck and rib bones as well as pork hocks. Pig ears and trotters are a good source of connective tissue and the much-needed cartilage that gives bone broth its body. Ham hocks, cured and smoked like bacon, also make a beautiful broth when combined with other foods, particularly earthy beans, but are too richly flavored to be used in the stockpot without something like lentils or beans to give them balance.

where to find bones for stocks and bone broths

You won't find pig ears and trotters, beef shin bones, veal knuckles, lamb neck bones, or chicken feet and necks in most supermarkets, but don't let lack of access to less familiar cuts keep you from making bone broths and stocks altogether; rather, use those cuts that are available until you can find a better source. You can often find bones tucked away in the bottom of the freezer case near the meat counter at grocery stores, and if you don't see them there, ask the butcher. Some supermarkets still butcher meat on site and might have soup bones available for customers who ask.

Many ethnic markets carry more exotic cuts of bone like trotters and chicken feet, as these shops typically cater to a clientele that doesn't share the squeamish American preference for de-animalized meats. Farmers' markets and farm stands also offer soup bones at fair and reasonable prices, but take care to ask your meat vendor in advance to bring them for you. Due to their relative lack of popularity and the limited space available to vendors at farmers' markets, some ranchers and farmers don't routinely stock them. You might also ask them, the next time you pick up a whole chicken, a steak, or a pound of ground meat, when they will process their animals next, reminding them to save bones that their processor might otherwise leave on the killing room floor: trotters, feet, knuckles, shins, neck and marrow bones. Specifying these bones, as opposed to the all-encompassing term *soup bones*, will ensure you receive a variety of bones for your soup pot.

wine or vinegar

The addition of something acidic, like wine or vinegar, not only helps build flavor in stocks and bone broths, but also facilitates the release of minerals from the bone. While bones are rich in minerals, bone broths are not necessarily a particularly good source of them, though they do contain a fair amount of calcium, magnesium, and potassium, especially given their high water content. Adding vinegar or wine to the cooking water helps the bones release those minerals. I favor wine over vinegar, owing mostly to its flavor, and so when I make bone broth, I add a glassful of wine to the pot and pour one to enjoy myself. I typically use dry white wine when preparing chicken stocks and broths, and red wine like Merlot or Cabernet Sauvignon when preparing beef stocks and bone broths.

vegetables you want (and those you don't)

Vegetables add flavor and depth to broths and stocks. Those flavors serve as the base notes on which you layer the middle and top notes of your dish, so be careful not to introduce flavors to your broth or stock that do not pair well with the flavors in your final dish. For this reason, and with the exception of vegetable broths, the stocks and broths included in this book are wonderfully bare, nothing more than bones, water, and wine. This allows you to season and flavor your broths and stocks as you see fit and ensure they will complement your final dish rather than detract from it.

Often the trimmings of whatever vegetables you happen to work with for dinner, or for a soup, work well to flavor your broth. If you're cooking with carrots, add the carrot tops and the peelings to flavor your broth, wasting as little of the vegetable in the process. The tough, fibrous stem of broccoli will flavor the base of a broccoli soup nicely, while a knob of ginger and the external layers of an onion can do wonders to flavor the broth of a curried butternut squash soup. Keep in mind that there are a few vegetables best avoided: Brassicas (aside from broccoli for a broccoli soup) like Brussels sprouts and cabbage can introduce bitter notes to stocks and broths, particularly during prolonged cooking. Beets and other root vegetables can be too earthy, and their carbohydrates break down during the long simmering time required of broths, resulting in broth that is too sweet.

In addition to helping broths and stocks develop flavor, vegetables also improve their mineral content. Vegetables easily part with their minerals and flavor when simmered in stocks and broths, so be sure to add them later in cooking than bones, which require more time to release their goodness. If added too early, vegetables can add undesirable strong, sweet notes to your stock or broth.

herbs and spices

Herbs and spices, like vegetables, help round out a broth's or stock's flavor. I often add whole peppercorns, bay leaves, thyme, and parsley to many of my broths and stocks. Or I might try a combination of ginger, lemongrass, and chile peppers for an Asian-inspired stock. A little goes a long way with herbs and spices, and too much can quickly overpower the flavor of a broth, especially with prolonged cooking. For home cooks who might use their broths and stocks in a variety of dishes with a sweeping array of flavor profiles, keeping the stock itself to little more than bones and water, and then seasoning only when you prepare your meal, is essential to ensure a great dish.

equipment for making broths and stocks

At its heart, making broth and stock is simple and uncomplicated, and this is also true of the necessary equipment. As long as you have a pot, you can make broth and stock. If you don't have them already, you might also invest in a Dutch oven, deep sauté pan, strainer, slow cooker, or pressure cooker, as your budget allows and your interest commands.

stockpot

Taller than it is wide, a stockpot is a straight-sided pot with a flat bottom. These dimensions allow it to conserve liquid as it simmers. As a result, you lose less of your broth to evaporation than you would in a wider pot, and its ample volume comfortably holds plenty of bones, even those long marrowbones and oddly shaped knuckle joints. Stockpots come in sizes that range from four quarts on the small end to twenty-four quarts on the large end. If you're an avid cook and have the room, you might invest in an eight-quart pot as well as a twelve-quart pot.

dutch oven

A Dutch oven is a squat, thick-walled pot typically made of cast iron or enameled cast iron, and because of their sturdy construction, they can go directly from the stove to the oven. Dutch ovens don't have the capacity of a large stockpot, but they're a good multipurpose pot for soups, stews, roasts, and dishes that make their own broth. I keep an enameled cast-iron six-quart Dutch oven handy for making pot roasts and soups.

fine-mesh sieve and a wide-mouth funnel

Once you've simmered your bones to the brink of disintegration, it's time to strain the broth. The best tools for straining broth are a fine-mesh sieve and a wide-mouth canning funnel. Set a wide-mouth funnel in a jar and then set a fine-mesh sieve over the funnel. Pour the broth through the sieve and into the jar to store it. Fine-mesh sieves are able to catch more bits of small bone and debris than colanders with wider holes, while wide-mouth canning funnels help you to pour broth from the pot into a jar or pitcher with greater ease and less opportunity for spills.

soup sock

Shaped like a bag, a thin cotton net soup sock allows you to stuff it full of your ingredients: bones, a chicken frame, vegetables, and herbs, as it suits you. Set the stuffed soup sock into your pot, pour enough water over it to cover, and simmer. When the stock finishes cooking, simply pull out the soup sock and discard the contents, and you're ready to go, no need to strain it.

deep sauté pan or reduction pan

When reducing stocks and broths to form thick, rich sauces, it's helpful to have a deep sauté pan with straight sides or a reduction pan. In contrast to the design of a tall, narrow stockpot, which limits evaporation, reduction pans, with their wide construction and shallow depth, promote quick evaporation, speeding the concentration of the stock.

skimmer

When making broths and stocks, protein and fat will rise to the surface of your pot, creating a gray-white foamy scum. While this foam is generally innocuous, it can turn your stock cloudy, making it look less appetizing. You can remove this scum with a skimmer, a tool that looks like a wide, flattened mesh ladle. Its shallow, wide surface area allows you to skim off all of the foam that surfaces, without losing much, if any, of the broth underneath.

immersion blender

Many soups benefit from blending, which can transform them from chunky to velvety and creamy. For these soups, I favor an immersion blender, also called a stick blender. An immersion blender is a long tool with two parts: the handle that also houses the motor and the blender that it powers. By submerging the blending blades into your soup pot, this tool allows you to blend and puree your food in the pot you've prepared it in.

other ways to make broth & stock

While making broth and stock on the stove top in a stockpot is easy, you can also make them in a pressure cooker, slow cooker, or the oven. Both pressure cookers and slow cookers will eliminate the time you might spend carefully monitoring the level of liquid in the pot, or in skimming off the foam that rises to the top of the stock as it simmers.

pressure cooker

A pressure cooker can speed up the otherwise long cooking process of making broth on the stove top, typically reducing cooking time by one-third. Once you've added your bones and any additional vegetables or herbs you like, cover them with liquid and pressure-cook the broth for about four hours.

slow cooker

Like a stockpot on the stove over low heat, the slow cooker keeps a low, even temperature, with the added blessing that it requires relatively little maintenance. Drop the bones into the slow cooker, cover them with water, and cook on low for twenty-four hours, then strain and use the broth as you normally would.

oven

Using the oven is an easy, low-maintenance way to make stock and bone broth. Ovens keep a slow, steady temperature that will keep the broth simmering ever so slightly until the bones soften, releasing their gelatin and minerals. Tuck the bones into a Dutch oven, cover them with water, and bring it to a boil on the stove over medium-high heat. Turn off the heat, transfer it to the oven, and leave the Dutch oven partially covered. Turn the oven to 200°F and continue cooking the broth, partially covered, for at least twelve, and up to twenty-four hours.

how to store broth & stock

While we seem to use up any broth and stock I make within a day or two, it's nice to have them on hand, readily stored, to use in a pinch. Reduction is my favorite storage method, as it concentrates flavor and shrinks the space required in the refrigerator. When I'm ready to use it, all I need to do is spoon a bit of the gelled broth or stock into a pot, add water, and heat it up. For those of you with little freezer space, lots of liquid, and a little time for experimentation, you might consider reducing them first and then drying

them in a dehydrator until they forms a firm, glassy sheet that you can then shatter or grind to a powder and rehydrate with a little water.

You can also freeze broth and stock easily. If you freeze them in ice cube trays, you can pull out just a few tablespoons at a time, rather than quarts.

Of course, one of the best ways to store homemade broth and stock is to pressure-can it, which allows you to store it for several years at room temperature.

reduction

To reduce a broth or stock, pour it into a wide and fairly shallow pan, like a sauté pan or a reduction pan. Bring to a simmer over medium-low heat so that it barely bubbles and then allow it to reduce until it is concentrated and viscous, like maple syrup.

The time it takes to reduce depends on three factors: the quantity of liquid you begin with, the type of pot you use, and how concentrated you like your final product to be. Reducing broth or stock in a wide and shallow pan takes less time, as the greater surface area hastens evaporation. You can concentrate it until reduced by half, becoming thin but syrupy, or you can reduce it further still until it reaches a viscous and ropy consistency like that needed for portable soup (page 93), an old-fashioned preserved broth. Pour your broth or stock into an airtight container and store it in the fridge for up to three weeks or in the freezer for up to six months.

dehydration

You can make your own instant stock powder, which is easily dissolved in hot water. First begin by reducing stock to one-tenth of its original volume in a wide, shallow pan set over medium-low heat. Allow it to cool to room temperature. While it cools, line the trays of a dehydrator with wax paper or ParaFlexx sheets. Spoon the cooled liquid onto the sheets, taking care to spoon no more than a cup onto each sheet. Dehydrate at 165°F for eighteen to twenty-four hours, or until it forms a brittle sheet. Break up the sheets of and then pulse in a food processor or spice grinder until they form a fine powder. Transfer to an airtight container and store at room temperature for up to one year.

freezing

For convenience, especially when you require only a small amount of broth at any given time, consider freezing the broth in small cubes. Pour room-temperature broth into ice cube trays, freeze them, break them out of the tray, and store in a resealable plastic freezer bag in the freezer for up to six months. Each cube will contain about two tablespoons of broth, for easy measurement into recipes. If you prefer to freeze larger quantities of broth and wish to avoid freezing your broth in plastic containers, remember that glass may crack or shatter while in the freezer. If you freeze in glass, be sure to keep the jars no more than three-quarters full.

pressure canning

If you plan to make large quantities of broth, you can pressure-can it. Pour the broth into quart-size glass canning jars and process in a weighted-gauge pressure canner at 10 PSI for twenty-five minutes for those of you living at an elevation of 1,000 feet or below, and process the jars at 15 PSI for twenty-five minutes for those of you living at an altitude above 1,000 feet. Always check with your local cooperative extension office for specific guidelines per your region. Pressure-canned broths and stocks will store for several years but should be used within one week once you open them. Broths and stocks are low-acid foods, and unlike pickles, jellies, and fruits, you cannot safely can them using the water bath method of submerging jars into boiling water until they seal; rather, broth and stock must be pressure-canned to eliminate the risk of food-borne illness like botulism. Pressure-canning broths and stocks can be particularly helpful for homesteaders or hunters who must process many pounds of bones all at once, but for most of us the process is laborious without offering many benefits.

At home, I favor keeping things simple. For me, it means relying on a few handy master recipes and reducing the broth or stock I make down to a fine gel, pouring it into an airtight container, and storing it in the fridge to use as needed. It is rhythms and routines like these, practiced until they become second nature, that keep the momentum flowing in my kitchen and provide me and my whole family comfort.

master broths and stocks

It always feels good to keep a few recipes that you know by heart tucked away to use when you need them. These master recipes provide the foundation on which you can build the rest of your cooking. With few ingredients in the pot, you build master broths and stocks that are neutral in flavor, allowing them to serve as the base for more complex dishes. You can flavor them as needed with vegetables, herbs, and spices to suit the dish you plan to make. Once prepared, you can use these broths and stocks immediately, or store them for later meals.

I always keep a bottle of wine in my kitchen, open and at the ready. I enjoy a glassful and pour a bit into the stockpot as I cook. Wine builds flavor into stocks and broths, complementing their natural, neutral, savory notes; it also performs a second purpose: softening the water and helping minerals to leach from the bones in your pot so they leave a trace of themselves in your broth. Beyond that, there's little more than water added. Once prepared, you can use the broth or stock immediately, or store it for later meals.

whole chicken broth

makes about 4 quarts, ready in 4 to 6 hours

1 whole chicken, 3 to 5 pounds

2 prepared chicken feet (see page 31), if available

¼ cup dry white wine

4–6 quarts cold water

A pale, straw-colored broth with a pronounced chicken flavor, whole chicken broth tastes of comfort. I like to use it as a base for brothy soups dotted with greens and fresh vegetables. It's also a wonderful time-saver because in addition to several quarts of broth, it also makes several cups of shredded, cooked chicken meat. You can add it to soups and casseroles or even make chicken salad with it.

....

Place the chicken in a large stockpot, toss in the prepared feet, and then pour in the wine. Pour in enough water to cover the bird by 1 inch (about 4–6 quarts). Cover the pot and bring to a boil over medium-high heat. Immediately lower the heat to medium-low and simmer, covered, for at least 4 and up to 6 hours, until the chicken meat is tender and separates easily from the bones.

Using a broth skimmer or mesh spoon, skim off and discard any foam that appears on the surface of the broth as it simmers (or reserve for Russian Chicken Skim Broth, page 50).

Turn off the heat. Gently remove the bird from the broth and allow it to cool until you can handle it comfortably. Carefully pick the meat off the bones. Place the meat in an airtight container and store it in the refrigerator for up to 5 days.

Strain the broth through a fine-mesh sieve and then use a wide-mouthed funnel to pour it into four 1-quart sized jars, sealing their lids tightly.

Cook with the broth right away or store it in the refrigerator for up to 1 week. Alternatively, you can freeze the broth for up to 6 months, making sure to allow plenty of headspace if you're using glass jars.

When you're ready to use your broth, spoon off any hardened fat at the top of the jar. You can reserve this fat to cook with, or discard it as it suits you.

chicken foot stock

makes about 4 quarts, ready in 8 to 12 hours

3 pounds prepared chicken feet (see opposite page)

¼ cup white wine

4–6 quarts cold water

Chicken feet are, perhaps, the last frontier for the broth maker. Unlike the neat plastic-wrapped packages of boneless, skinless chicken breasts you find in the grocery store, chicken feet are decidedly and unrepentantly animalistic. If they make you squeamish, I don't blame you. If you can transcend their ick factor long enough to drop chicken feet into a stockpot, you'll reap the rewards in a resolutely flavor-rich, silky stock, dense with gelatin.

....

Place the chicken feet into a heavy stockpot, pour in the wine, and add enough cold water to cover the chicken feet by 1 inch (about 4–6 quarts). Cover the pot, bring to a boil over medium-high heat, and then immediately turn down the heat to medium-low. Keep the feet at a bare simmer, uncovered, for at least 8 and up to 12 hours, adding water as necessary to keep the feet submerged. Skim off any foam that appears on the surface of the broth and discard it.

Strain the broth through a fine-mesh sieve. Discard the spent feet, as you won't need them after you've made the stock.

Use the stock right away or transfer into four 1-quart sized jars, sealing their lids tightly. Alternatively, you can freeze the stock for up to 6 months, making sure to allow plenty of headspace if you're using glass jars.

A thin layer of yellow fat may rise to the surface of your refrigerated or frozen stock and harden; spoon off and discard the fat before cooking with the stock. Unlike the fat rendered from bone broths and other stocks, the fat rendered from chicken feet doesn't lend itself well to other uses in the kitchen.

how to prepare chicken feet

You can find chicken feet at many ethnic grocers, health food stores, and even at farmers' markets and farm stands if you request them ahead of time so your rancher knows to save them at the time she culls her flock. For the most part, when you purchase chicken feet, they will already be prepared, but if not here is how I prepare them at home.

A thin, papery yellow membrane adheres to chicken feet. When left on the feet, and in the stockpot, it can create more scum that you'll need to skim and even introduce off-flavors to the stock, so it's best to remove the membrane. Working with feet that have been frozen first helps you to remove that membrane more easily.

To prepare chicken feet, bring a pot of water to a rolling boil over high heat. While the water comes to a boil, prepare an ice bath by dumping a few cupfuls of ice into a large mixing bowl and filling it half full with cold water.

To prevent crowding and overcooking, drop one chicken foot at a time into the boiling water. Leave it in for a second or two, then transfer it to the ice bath with tongs. Continue this process until you've put all of the chicken feet in the ice bath.

Just as the skin of a tomato or peach will separate easily from the fruit when first put into boiling water and then into ice water, so too will the membrane on the chicken foot loosen. Take the chicken feet from the ice water and gently pull away the membrane from each foot and discard it.

Now, lay each foot on a sturdy cutting board and chop off each talon at the first joint with a sharp knife. This practice helps you to keep a clearer broth. Once you've removed the membranes and talons, your chicken feet are ready for the stockpot.

chicken bone broth

makes about 4 quarts, ready in 8 to 18 hours

The spent frame of 1 roasted chicken, like the one on page 60

½ cup dry white wine

4–6 quarts cold water

I plunk the bones of a roasted chicken into my stockpot about once a week where it simmers away for hours, producing a beautiful, rich golden broth with deep savory notes marked by hints of caramel. Clear and delicate, it's nice sipped on its own or used as a base for soups dotted with vegetables and fortified by grains or starchy potatoes.

....

Drop the bones in a stockpot, add the wine and then cover the bones with water by about 1-inch (4-6 quarts). Bring to a boil over medium-high heat, then immediately turn down to medium-low, and simmer, covered, for at least 8 and up to 18 hours, or until the broth is rich and fragrant and the bones crumble when you press them between your thumb and forefinger. Skim off any foam that rises to the top of the stockpot as necessary. Reserve the foam for Russian Chicken Skim Broth (page 50) or discard it.

Strain the broth through a fine-mesh sieve and then use a wide-mouthed funnel to pour it into four 1-quart jars, sealing their lids tightly. Cook with the broth right away or place the jars in the refrigerator for up to one week. Alternatively you can freeze the broth for up to 6 months, making sure to allow plenty of headspace if you're using glass jars.

When you're ready to serve the broth, you'll notice a thin layer of semisolid yellow fat at the top of the jar. Spoon off this fat and use the broth as you would normally. You can reserve the fat to use as you would any cooking fat or try it in Schmaltz Mashed Potatoes and Gravy with Black Pepper and Fresh Thyme (page 63).

roasted turkey bone broth

makes about 4 quarts, ready in 14 to 24 hours

The spent frame of
1 roasted turkey

4 carrots, sliced 1 inch thick

6 celery stalks, sliced
1 inch thick

1 large yellow onion,
quartered and unpeeled

2 bay leaves

1 tablespoon whole
black peppercorns

½ cup dry white wine

4–6 quarts cold water

Each spring we reserve a turkey, or sometimes two, from a farmer. We visit her farm to pick up our weekly share of vegetables, and we always take the time to visit our turkey, too. It grows quickly at first, and then, just in time for Thanksgiving, it's plump enough for the dinner table. I like to marinate it in a brine made of sweet apple cider, salt, sugar, and spices for a few days, before slow-roasting it overnight. We serve it to our hungry guests, and after we've picked as much meat off the bones as we can, I toss the turkey's bones into the soup pot with aromatic vegetables, bay leaves, and black pepper to make a rich, golden-colored bone broth that serves as a base for soups that will nourish us for a week after Thanksgiving.

....

Place the turkey bones into a large stockpot and then add the carrots and celery. Arrange the onion in the pot with the turkey bones and vegetables. Toss in the bay leaves and peppercorns and then pour in the wine and water. Bring it all to a boil over medium-high heat, and then immediately lower the heat to medium-low and simmer, covered, for at least 14 and up to 24 hours, until the bones crumble when crushed. Skim off and discard any foam that rises to the top of the stockpot as necessary.

Strain the broth through a fine-mesh sieve, and then use a wide-mouthed funnel to pour it into four 1-quart jars, sealing their lids tightly. Cook with the broth right away or store it in the refrigerator for up to 1 week. Alternatively, you can freeze the broth for up to 6 months, making sure to allow plenty of headspace if you're using glass jars.

When you're ready to serve the broth, you'll notice a thin layer of semisolid yellow fat at the top of the jar. Spoon off the fat, which you can reserve and use to sauté or roast vegetables, or discard it, then use the broth as a base for turkey gravy or in Turkey Soup with Root Vegetables and Wild Rice (page 75).

long-simmered roasted
beef bone broth

makes about 4 quarts, ready in 12 to 18 hours

5 pounds beef soup bones, such as neck and marrow bones or knuckles and shins

1 cup red wine

4–6 quarts cold water

When we order our beef, once a year, straight from a nearby rancher who raises his steers on grassy rangeland, we make sure to order soup bones. We also ask the butcher to reserve knuckles and cartilage-rich cuts of bone that he might normally discard. A combination of meaty neck bones, fatty marrowbones, and joints work well to create a broth that is at once flavorsome, luxuriant, and silky in texture, producing a solid, bouncing gel when cooled. You can read more about where to order these bones on page 172.

…………

Preheat the oven to 425°F.

Place the bones in a single layer in a roasting pan and roast in the heated oven for 45 minutes.

Transfer the bones to a heavy stockpot and then pour in the wine. Add enough water to cover the bones by 2 inches (about 4–6 quarts).

Bring the liquid to a boil over high heat, and then immediately lower the heat to medium-low. Cover and simmer for at least 12 and up to 18 hours, adding water as necessary to keep the bones submerged.

Strain the broth through a fine-mesh sieve and then use a wide-mouthed funnel to pour it into four 1-quart jars, sealing their lids tightly. Cook with the broth right away or place the jars in the refrigerator to allow the fat to harden. Alternatively, you can freeze the broth for up to 6 months, making sure to allow plenty of headspace if you're using glass jars. Be sure to spoon off the hard layer of fat before cooking with the broth. You can reserve this fat to cook with, or discard it as it suits you.

fat from bone broths and stocks

As bones and the connective tissue that adheres to them simmer in water to produce a rich stock or bone broth, they release proteins, minerals, and fat. The fat renders, and just as cream rises to the surface of non-homogenized milk, so too does fat rise to the surface of stocks and bone broths, solidifying as it cools.

Fat acts as a preservative, and has been used to help preserve foods for millennia. When fat rises to the surface and hardens as bone broths and stocks cool, it forms a seal that helps to preserve the broth, ensuring that its flavor is maintained for a week or so in the fridge.

Once you're ready to use your stock or bone broth, you can break that seal of fat, and pour out the liquid. Save the rendered fat at the surface of your refrigerated stocks and bone broths and use it for cooking.

Schmaltz, or rendered chicken fat, offers a rich and deep chicken flavor. It is rich in monounsaturated fat which gives it a softer, semisolid texture once it renders. You can use it in Schmaltz Mashed Potatoes and Gravy (page 63) or spoon it over root vegetables before you set them to roast in a hot oven.

Tallow, or rendered beef fat, is a particularly hard fat, owing to its high saturated fat content. Use it to pan-fry vegetables and meats or in Tallow-Roasted Onions with Fresh Rosemary (page 168).

Lard, or rendered pork fat, is semisolid, like schmaltz, with a mild pork flavor. Lard gets a bad rap, very much undeserved, and it may surprise you to learn that the dominant fat in lard is monunsaturated, the same "heart healthy" fat found in olive oil and avocados. Use lard for frying, for roasting vegetables, or as a replacement for butter in baking.

long-simmered roasted pork bone broth

makes about 4 quarts, ready in 8 to 16 hours

5 pounds pork bones, such as neck bones and trotters

1 cup red wine

4–6 quarts cold water

Where chicken bone broths are light, and beef bone broths are assertive, pork broth falls somewhere in between. Depending on the breed of the pig, your pork bones may render a great deal of fat or very little. Heritage breeds, like Mangalitsa, tend to produce more fat than modern breeds. You can spoon off the fat that rises to the surface of your broth as it cools and use it just as you might any other cooking fat, though it is particularly nice for sautéing onions or in biscuits and piecrust.

Take care not to choose smoked pork hock or ham hocks for a basic broth like this, as they will impart their smoky flavor into the liquid, which may or may not benefit your final dish. Instead, use smoked pork hock or ham hocks in dishes like Galician Pork and Bean Stew with Greens (page 105) or Pinto Beans and Ham Hock (page 116).

....

Preheat the oven to 425°F.

Place the bones in a roasting pan in a single layer and roast them in the heated oven for 45 minutes, or until they render a bit of fat and their edges begin to caramelize a little.

Transfer the bones to a heavy stockpot and then pour in the wine. Add enough water to cover the bones by 2 inches (about 4–6 quarts).

Bring the liquid to a boil over high heat, and then immediately lower the heat to medium-low. Cover and simmer for at least 8 and up to 16 hours, adding water as necessary to keep the bones fully submerged.

Strain the broth through a fine-mesh sieve and then use a wide-mouthed funnel to pour it into four 1-quart jars, sealing their lids tightly. Cook with the broth right away or store it in the refrigerator for up to 1 week. Alternatively, you can freeze the broth for up to 6 months, making sure to allow plenty of headspace if you're using glass jars. If refrigerated or frozen scoop off the fat and reserve as a cooking fat for Pork Pot Roast with Sweet Potato, Ancho Chile, and Lime (page 119).

fish stock

makes about 4-6 quarts, ready in 25 minutes

5 pounds fish trimmings, such as the bones and head

1 cup dry white wine

4-6 quarts cold water

Fish are delicate creatures and do not withstand prolonged cooking well. Heat can damage their fragile polyunsaturated fatty acids, leaving the stock with an overly fishy off-flavor. Their thin and almost translucent bones don't need as much coaxing to release their nutrients as beef bones do, and so just a short while in the pot, less than an hour, is sufficient to give you a good, nutritive fish stock.

When making fish stock, it's best to avoid oily fish like salmon, mackerel, Arctic char, and sardines, as their fragile oils can break down easily with the prolonged exposure to heat required in making stock, leaving an unpleasant flavor. Instead, choose the frames of nonoily fish like cod, plaice, haddock, snapper, or catfish to make your stock, as they'll impart a better flavor.

If you don't fish yourself, you can purchase whole fish or fish trimmings. Fishmongers and natural foods markets with fish counters will often sell you the bones and heads at very affordable rates or give them to you if you ask.

. . . .

Drop the fish trimmings into a heavy stockpot and then pour in the wine. Cover with cold water by 1 inch (about 4-6 quarts) and then slowly bring the broth to a bare simmer over medium heat. Skim off and discard any foam or scum that rises to the surface of the stock and discard. Simmer the stock for about 25 minutes, or until fragrant but not overpowering.

Strain the stock through a fine-mesh sieve and use it right away or store it in four 1-quart sized jars, sealing their lids tightly, for no more than 5 days. Alternatively you can freeze the stock for up to 6 months, making sure to allow plenty of headspace if you're using glass jars.

dashi

makes about 3 cups, ready in 15 to 20 minutes

4 cups cold water

1 (6-inch) strip kombu

1 cup bonito flakes

A traditional base for soups in Japan, dashi is made from seaweed and bonito flakes, or shaved flakes of dried skipjack tuna, which you can find at many supermarkets and health foods stores as well as Asian markets. Mild in flavor, dashi makes for a clear broth with faint, subtle notes of smoke and fish.

I like to keep dashi on hand, tucked in the back of my fridge, so that I can pull it out at any moment and make a fast miso soup or use it to braise vegetables like the Miso-Glazed Bok Choy (page 149).

....

Fill a saucepan with the water and drop in a strip of kombu. Bring to a bare simmer over medium-high heat and then pluck out the kombu with a pair of tongs and discard it. Stir the bonito flakes into the hot water. Turn off the heat and cover the pot. Let the pot sit undisturbed until all of the bonito flakes sink to the bottom of the saucepan, about 10 minutes.

Strain the broth through a fine-mesh sieve, discarding the solids. Use the dashi immediately, or pour it into a 1-quart jar with a tight-fitting lid and store it in the fridge for up to 5 days or in the freezer for up to 6 months, making sure to allow plenty of headspace if you're using glass jars.

shellfish stock

makes about 2 quarts, ready in 60 to 65 minutes

1 pound shellfish shells, such as the shells of shrimp, lobster, and crab

1 cup dry white wine

2–4 quarts cold water

Unlike meat stocks and broths, shellfish shells, which form the base for this stock, are not particularly rich in protein, so they will not yield as firm a gel; rather, these shells are rich in trace minerals, notably selenium, which acts as an antioxidant while also supporting thyroid function. If you have just shelled shrimp or other shellfish, you can make this stock right away. You can also toss shells into a resealable plastic bag, store them in the freezer for up to 6 months, and pull it out when you need to make stock.

....

Preheat the oven to 400°F.

Arrange the shellfish shells in a single layer on a baking sheet and roast them in the heated oven until they turn crisp and brown at the edges, about 20 minutes.

Remove the baking sheet from the oven and transfer the shells to a heavy stockpot. Stir in the wine. Cover with water by 1 inch (about 2–4 quarts) and then slowly bring the broth to a bare simmer over medium heat. Skim off and discard any foam or scum that rises to the surface of the stock. Simmer the stock for about 45 minutes, or until fragrant but not overpowering.

Strain the stock through a fine-mesh sieve and use it right away or store it in two 1-quart jars, sealed tightly in the fridge for no more than 5 days. Alternatively, you can freeze the stock for up to 6 months, making sure to allow plenty of headspace if you're using glass jars.

green broth

makes about 2 quarts, ready in 20 to 25 minutes

1 bunch parsley, coarsely chopped

1 bunch kale, coarsely chopped

1 bunch watercress, coarsely chopped

3 celery stalks, coarsely chopped

4 green onions, coarsely chopped

6 cloves garlic, coarsely chopped

1 (6-inch) strip kombu

2–3 quarts cold water or Whole Chicken Broth (page 28)

Adding vegetables, particularly leafy greens, to broth infuses it with not only bright vegetal notes but also minerals. While you can make a basic vegetable stock with nothing more than vegetables and water, you can also substitute the whole chicken broth as a base instead of water. This combination results in a broth rich in flavor as well as in protein and minerals like calcium, magnesium, phosphorus, potassium, and manganese. You can use any variety of kale you happen to find at the market or sprouting up in your garden for this recipe, including curly kale, purple kale, and Lacinato kale. This broth can be enjoyed plain, with a sprinkling of sea salt, or used as a base for soups where its vibrant, green, and almost grassy notes bring added complexity.

....

Add the parsley, kale, watercress, celery, onions, and garlic to a stockpot. Pour in 2–3 quarts of water or chicken broth and drop the kombu into the pot. Bring the whole thing to a bare simmer over medium-high heat and continue cooking, covered, for 20 minutes, or until the liquid takes on a pale yellow-green hue.

Strain the broth through a fine-mesh sieve, and then use a wide-mouthed funnel to pour it into two 1-quart jars, sealing the lids tightly. Cook with the broth right away or store it in the refrigerator for no more than 5 days. Alternatively, you can freeze the broth for up to 6 months, making sure to allow plenty of headspace if you're using glass jars.

roasted mushroom broth

makes about 2 quarts, ready in 60 to 65 minutes

¾ pound mixed mushrooms or mushroom stems, chopped into ½-inch pieces

1 yellow onion, skin on and halved crosswise

3 cloves garlic, smashed

1 tablespoon olive oil

2 quarts cold water or Chicken Bone Broth (page 32)

¼ cup dry white wine

6 sprigs thyme

Roasting strengthens the flavor of mushrooms, amplifying the savory and almost meaty base notes that can give soups a unique foundational richness. Those savory flavors serve as a good match for meat and whole grains. Use this broth as a base for mushroom soups and stews or in risottos and pilafs. Using a wide variety of mushrooms will improve this broth's flavor and complexity. I often use the stems and trimmings of wild mushrooms left over from foraging, as they give the broth a remarkable depth of flavor; however, using the button or cremini mushrooms easily available year-round in most grocery stores also yields a lovely broth, as roasting improves their flavor. You don't need to take the peel off the onion, as it produces a lovely color, just split the onion in half and drop it in the pot.

....

Preheat the oven to 425°F.

Arrange the mushrooms in a single layer on a baking sheet. Nestle the onion halves into the mushrooms, sprinkle the smashed garlic over, and drizzle with the olive oil. Roast for 20 minutes in the heated oven.

Remove the sheet from the oven and drop the roasted mushrooms and onions into a heavy stockpot. Pour in the broth and wine. Slip the sprigs of thyme into the pot and then bring it all to a simmer over medium-high heat. Continue simmering, covered, for about 30 minutes.

Strain the broth through a fine-mesh sieve, then use a wide-mouthed funnel to pour it into two 1-quart jars, sealing the lids tightly. Cook with the broth right away or store it in the refrigerator for no more than 5 days. Alternatively, you can freeze the broth for up to 6 months, making sure to allow plenty of headspace if you're using glass jars.

sea vegetable broth

makes about 2 quarts, ready in 25 to 30 minutes

6 green onions, chopped into 1-inch pieces

2 celery stalks, chopped into 1-inch pieces

1 carrot, chopped into 1-inch pieces

1 (6-inch) strip kombu

1 leaf dried dulse

8 dried shiitakes

2–3 quarts cold water or Whole Chicken Broth (page 28)

Sea vegetables are among my favorite foods and are extraordinarily rich in minerals, particularly iodine, which helps support thyroid health. Dried seaweed is available for purchase in many natural foods stores. Kombu comes in long, thick, brittle strips that soften readily in warm water. Dulse, by contrast, is leafy and thin, breaking easily into flakes, which is how it is often sold. For this recipe, purchase dried dulse leafs, not dulse flakes, which will filter through your sieve when you try to strain your broth.

Drop the onions, celery, and carrot into a heavy stockpot. Check the kombu and dulse leaves for any stray shells or debris that might adhere to them, and then add them to the pot with the veggies. Add the shiitakes to the pot, pour in the water, and bring to a bare simmer over medium-high heat. Turn down the heat to medium and simmer, covered, for 20 minutes.

Strain the broth through a fine-mesh sieve, then use a wide-mouthed funnel to pour it into two 1-quart jars, sealing the lids tightly. Cook with the broth right away or store it in the refrigerator for no more than 5 days. Alternatively, you can freeze the broth for up to 6 months, making sure to allow plenty of headspace if you're using glass jars.

double-cooked stock (remouillage)

makes about 2 quarts, ready in 6 to 8 hours

The spent bones from
a batch of stock or
bone broth

1/2 cup red or white wine,
or as needed

2-3 quarts cold water

After you've prepared your stock, strained it, and sealed it in jars
for storage, you'll find yourself left with a heaping mess of softened
bones. You can certainly discard these, but you might also take a
lesson from the French, who make a traditional, double-cooked stock
using bones that have already been simmered once. *Remouillage* is
weaker in flavor than a stock made with bones used for the first time,
but you'll still extract some flavor, some protein, and trace minerals
a second time, too, helping you waste even less in the kitchen. Owing
to its lighter, less concentrated flavor, *remouillage* works well in dishes
where other flavors dominate and in place of water in vegetable broths.

....

Toss the spent bones back into the stockpot, adding up to 1/2 cup wine,
as it suits you. Cover the bones with water by 2 inches (about 2–3 quarts)
and bring to a boil over medium-high heat. Immediately lower the heat
to medium-low and let the bones simmer, covered, for up to 8 hours.

Strain the stock through a fine-mesh sieve, then use a wide-mouthed
funnel to pour it into two 1-quart jars, sealing the lids tightly. Cook
with the stock right away or store it in the refrigerator for no more
than 5 days. Alternatively, you can freeze the stock for up to 6 months,
making sure to allow plenty of headspace if you're using glass jars.

russian chicken skim broth (pena)

makes about 4 cups, ready in 2 to 3 hours

4 cups Chicken Bone Broth (page 32) or Whole Chicken Broth (page 28)

Reserved foam from Chicken Bone Broth (page 32) or Whole Chicken Broth (page 28)

Most recipes for broths and stocks, including those within the pages of this cookbook, will invariably instruct you to remove the foamy scum that rises to the surface of the bubbling pot as it cooks, noting that this scum is full of impurities.

The foam that rises to the top of your stock and bone broth as it simmers away is in fact only impure in a culinary sense, as the proteins and fats that make up that foam can cloud your stock and potentially shorten the length of time it will last in your fridge. However, there's nothing actually harmful about it. Russian homemakers from generations past found a use for this foamy scum, skimming it away and then reconstituting it to form *pena*, a fortified broth. This recipe is adapted from the nineteenth century book on classical Russian cooking, *A Gift to Young Housewives*, by Elena Molokhevets.

....

The next time you prepare Chicken Bone Broth or Whole Chicken Broth, keep a small saucepan on the back of the stove. Spoon any foam that rises to the surface of your broth into the saucepan.

Once you've finished preparing your broth, reserve 4 cups of it. Pour the reserved broth into a saucepan. Stir in the reserved chicken broth foam that sits at the back of your stove into the broth and then cover the saucepan. Bring to a bare simmer over medium heat and then turn down the heat to low. The foam will dissolve into the broth, fortifying it as it does. Allow the broth to cook covered and undisturbed for 2 hours and then use it for any recipe that calls for chicken broth or serve it on its own seasoned with salt and pepper.

If you're not using right away, strain the broth through a fine-mesh sieve then use a wide-mouthed funnel to pour it into a 1-quart jar, sealing the lid tightly. Store in the refrigerator for up to 1 week. Alternatively, you can freeze the broth for up to 6 months, making sure to allow plenty of headspace if you're using a glass jar.

kitchen scrap broth

makes about 4 quarts, ready in 8 to 12 hours

2 to 3 pounds leftover chicken bones or chicken scraps like necks, backs, and wings

2½ cups loosely packed vegetable trimmings, such as onion skins, carrot peelings, celery leaves, and parsley stems

2 dried bay leaves

1 tablespoon whole black peppercorns

2 tablespoons white wine vinegar

4–6 quarts cold water

If there's one thing I loathe in the kitchen, it is waste.

I reserve carrot greens and peelings, onion skins, celery leaves, and herbs, tucking them away in a glass casserole dish with a tight-fitting lid that I keep in the freezer. Once I've filled it up, I know it's time to pair it with bones and make my kitchen scrap broth. When saving vegetable trimmings for broth, I favor mild- and clean-flavored vegetables like carrots, parsnips, celery, celeriac, and fresh herbs.

Brassicas, like broccoli, cabbage, kale, and collards, can infuse the broth with undesirable bitter notes, so it's best to avoid them. Too many roots, like beets, can leave your broth oddly sweet with a subtle but unnerving metallic finish.

....

Dump all of the ingredients into a heavy stockpot and then pour enough water into the pot to cover by 1 inch (about 4–6 quarts). Cover the pot and bring it to a boil over medium-high heat. Immediately turn down the heat to medium-low and simmer for at least 8 and up to 12 hours, skimming the broth as needed, until the bones crumble when you pinch them between your thumb and forefinger.

Strain the broth through a fine-mesh sieve, then use a wide-mouthed funnel to pour it into four 1-quart jars, sealing the lids tightly. Cook with the broth right away or store it in the refrigerator for no more than 5 days. Alternatively, you can freeze the broth for up to 6 months, making sure to allow plenty of headspace if you're using glass jars.

poultry

There's a healing beauty in a bowl of chicken broth, all golden and steaming. It can nurse you through a wicked cold, warm you on a cold winter day, and provide the elusive magic ingredient whose flavor enhances even the most basic of dinners. In my household, I keep chicken stock handy nearly all the time, sometimes warming it in a mug for Morning Broth (page 56), or tossing it into pan to bring moisture to vegetables as they braise. It's perpetually there, ready and willing to serve. The recipes in this chapter showcase the incredible versatility of poultry broth and stocks.

For those of you new to making homemade broths and stocks, chicken is, perhaps, the best first choice. The ingredients for chicken broth are readily available in nearly every grocery store or at any farmers' market, it requires no involved or complicated cooking, and it yields nearly universally appealing results.

morning broth

serves 1

¾ cup Chicken Bone Broth (page 32)

Leaves from 3 sprigs flat-leaf parsley, minced

1 clove garlic, minced

Coarse sea salt

I've never been one for coffee. Instead, most mornings I begin my day with a mug of broth. It fortifies me for the day ahead and hydrates me from the long night before. I like to drop in a few minced leaves of flat-leaf parsley and a clove of garlic, always with a sprinkling of finely ground sea salt. Freshly grated ginger and turmeric do nicely in a morning broth, too.

....

Warm the broth in a small saucepan set over medium-high heat. When tiny bubbles begin to creep up the sides of the saucepan, drop in the parsley and garlic and sprinkle enough salt into the broth to suit your taste. Pour into a mug and serve warm.

Variations: If you don't care for parsley and garlic, you can season your broth in any way that suits you. I've listed some of my favorite combinations below.

Turmeric and Ginger: Grate a ½-inch knob of fresh turmeric and a ½-inch knob of fresh ginger and then swirl it in with a spoon. Let it sit for 4 or 5 minutes to let the flavors marry and then drink the broth warm.

Garlic, Egg Yolk, and Parmesan: Mince a clove of garlic and stir it into your broth along with a single egg yolk and 2 tablespoons of finely grated Parmesan cheese.

Green Onion, Ginger, and Chile: Thinly slice the white, light green, and green parts of a single green onion and then grate a ½-inch knob of peeled ginger. Stir both into your mug and top it with a single slice of serrano pepper or jalapeño.

broth for infants

makes about 4 cups

1 pound boneless, skinless chicken thighs, finely chopped (no larger than 1/2 inch)

Long considered a healing food, meat-based broths like this one were thought to provide particularly valuable nourishment to those recovering from illness and to infants just beginning solid foods as an adjunct to breast milk. Many centuries-old American cookbooks and housekeeping guides include broth recipes for infants, some of which include mutton, but most of which include chicken, like the one below that I've adapted from *Jennie June*'s *American Cookery Book*, published in 1870.

Lacking the gelatin and mineral content of bone broths and stocks, meat-based broths like this one provide hydration, a touch of flavor, and a bit of protein. You can sip it on its own, as these broths were intended to be consumed, or use it as a base for soups or purees. If you intend to serve this to your own baby or toddler, take care not to salt the broth too heavily, as little bodies tend not to benefit from too much salt. Remember to serve it as it was traditionally served: as an addition to breast milk and other foods, not a replacement for them.

....

Drop the meat into a 1-quart jar and then cover it with cold water up to the neck of the jar. Seal the lid tightly. Place the jar on a rack in a stockpot. Pour enough water into the stockpot to cover the top of the jar by 1 inch. Bring the water in the stockpot to boil over medium-high heat and then turn down the heat to medium. Simmer for 6 hours, then remove the jar from the pot and allow it to cool until you can handle it comfortably.

Open up the jar carefully. Strain the liquid through a fine-mesh sieve, discarding the solids, into a second jar or storage container. Serve the broth right away or store it in an airtight container in the refrigerator up to 1 week.

slow-roasted salt and pepper chicken

serves 6

1 lemon, quartered

1 yellow onion, unpeeled and quartered

1 whole chicken, 3 to 5 pounds

2 tablespoons extra-virgin olive oil

2 heaping tablespoons coarse sea salt

1 teaspoon freshly ground black pepper

½ cup dry white wine

Once a week, usually on Sundays, we take the time to roast a whole chicken. Roasted for several hours at a low temperature, rather than fast and hot, poultry turns wonderfully luscious, with fork-tender meat that falls off the bone when carved. Don't be put off by the two tablespoons of salt called for in this recipe; it helps crisp the skin and seal moisture into the breast meat. If it's too salty for your liking, simply brush off any excess salt before you serve it.

....

Tuck the bird's wings behind its back and then stuff its cavity with the lemon and onion quarters. (Both the lemon and onion lend a bit of moisture to the bird as it roasts, ensuring that it doesn't dry out during the several hours it spends in the oven.) Tie the legs together with cotton cooking twine. Gently place it in an ovenproof 6-quart Dutch oven. Drizzle olive oil over the chicken, and then sprinkle it with the salt and pepper. Pour ½ cup of the wine into the bottom of the Dutch oven.

Cover the pot and set it in the oven on the middle rack. Turn the oven to 275°F. Roast the bird for 3 hours, taking care not to disturb it as it cooks. Remove the lid, turn the heat up to 375°F, and continue roasting it for 45 minutes more, or until the skin crisps to a lovely amber brown.

Remove the chicken from the oven and allow it to rest in the pot for 10 minutes. Place the chicken on a carving board or platter and carve into individual portions: breasts, thighs, and drumsticks, saving as much meat as possible and reserve the bones for Chicken Bone Broth (page 32). Serve the chicken immediately, as it makes a nice dinner with accompaniments of vegetables and potatoes.

schmaltz mashed potatoes and gravy
with black pepper and fresh thyme

serves 6

For the Potatoes

1 1/2 pounds Yukon gold potatoes, peeled and quartered

2 tablespoons coarsely ground sea salt

1/4 cup schmaltz

1 cup Chicken Bone Broth (page 32)

For the Gravy

4 cups Chicken Bone Broth (page 32)

2 tablespoons schmaltz

1/4 cup flour

1/2 teaspoon fresh thyme leaves

1 teaspoon freshly ground black pepper

Finely ground sea salt

There is something inherently comforting about curling up to a bowl of mashed potatoes swimming in toffee-colored, salty gravy. Schmaltz, soft and pale yellow, is rendered chicken fat, popular in traditional Ashkenazi Jewish cooking. It offers a delicate but pronounced chicken flavor, and owing to its high monounsaturated fat content, it makes an excellent and versatile cooking fat. Its flavor pairs well with other neutral ingredients like potatoes, offering a lovely alternative to butter. You can buy rendered schmaltz in some specialty grocery stores as well as online, or you can simply spoon the fat that rises to the top of your homemade chicken stock into a jar in your refrigerator, where it will harden, and save it for this recipe.

Make the potatoes: Drop the potatoes into a large stockpot and cover them with water by 2 inches. Stir in the salt and bring the potatoes to a boil over high heat. Boil, covered, until the potatoes soften and become tender, about 30 minutes.

Make the gravy: While the potatoes cook, pour the broth into a saucepan over medium heat. As the broth warms, blend the schmaltz and flour together in a small bowl with the back of a fork or a pastry blender until it forms a paste.

When you see the tiniest of bubbles appear on the sides of the saucepan, drop about 1 teaspoon of the schmaltz paste into the broth. Whisk it furiously into the broth until no lumps remain and then continue working the paste into the broth about 1 teaspoon at a time until you've used it all. Continue whisking the gravy until thickened to your liking. Stir in the thyme and black pepper and season with salt.

continued

Turn down the temperature to its lowest setting and keep the gravy warm while you finish the potatoes.

Once the potatoes are tender, drain them, and then transfer them to a stand mixer fitted with the paddle attachment. Spoon in the schmaltz and beat until it melts and absorbs into the potatoes. Beat the broth into the potatoes a few tablespoons at a time until the potatoes fully absorb the broth and whip them together until smooth, with no lumps remaining. Season with salt and pepper as you like it.

Spoon the potatoes into a serving bowl and serve them with the gravy.

chicken soup with parmesan, rice, peas, and lemon

serves 6 to 8

4 ounces Parmesan cheese, with the rind

½ cup long-grain white rice

2 tablespoons butter

1 leek, halved and sliced about ¼ inch thick

3 celery stalks, chopped into ¼-inch cubes

1 cup cooked, shredded chicken

6 cups Whole Chicken Broth (page 28)

1 cup fresh or frozen shelled green peas

Juice and zest of 1 lemon

1 small bunch flat-leaf parsley, coarsely chopped

Finely ground sea salt

Freshly ground black pepper

I like to make this soup during the few weeks when winter transitions to spring, pairing the last of winter's Meyer lemons with the first of spring's leeks and peas. These three ingredients are combined with rice and flat-leaf parsley for a comforting, brothy soup that has a vibrant, tart finish. The rind of a spent wedge of Parmesan cheese yields a creamy, faintly salty richness to the broth when plopped into the simmering soup pot. If you don't happen to have Meyer lemons, a standard lemon will do fine.

I always serve this soup with a big salad of spring vegetables and herbs: buttercrunch lettuce, thinly sliced radishes, mint, chervil, chives, and edible flowers like calendula and snapdragon, if the garden happens to provide them.

. . . .

Grate the Parmesan cheese very finely, reserving the rind. Pour the rice into a fine-mesh sieve and rinse it under the faucet until the water runs clear. Set the sieve holding the rice over a bowl, so that it continues to drain while you prepare the other ingredients.

Melt the butter in a heavy stockpot over medium-high heat. When it froths, add the rice to the pot, sautéing it in the hot fat until the tips of the grains become translucent, about 2 minutes. Toss the sliced leek and chopped celery into the pot, stirring continuously until the vegetables soften and release their aroma, about 3 minutes. Stir in the cooked chicken and cook for 2 minutes more.

continued

Pour the broth into the soup pot and then drop in the Parmesan rind. Bring to a simmer, and then turn down the heat to medium. If you're using fresh peas, stir the peas into the broth after the rice has cooked for about 10 minutes. Continue to simmer the soup, covered, until both the rice and the fresh peas are tender, about 10 minutes further. If you're using frozen peas, simply cook the rice until tender, 15 to 20 minutes, and then stir the frozen peas into the soup, continuing to simmer until they're warmed through, about 5 minutes more.

Turn off the heat. Using a pair of tongs, pluck out the Parmesan rind and discard it. Pour the lemon juice through a fine-mesh strainer to remove any seeds and into the soup. Sprinkle in the parsley and lemon zest. Taste the soup, adjusting its seasoning with salt and pepper as it suits you. Ladle the soup into bowls and top with grated Parmesan cheese just before serving.

the chicken soup cure

Anyone who has sequestered themselves away in bed, fighting off the sniffles and a scratchy throat, knows the comfort that chicken soup brings. Traditional wisdom promises that chicken soup will cure a cold, and the reputation of its medicinal benefits goes back hun-dreds of years. In the tenth century, the Persian physician Avicenna remarked on chicken soup's curative properties, and centuries later Maimonides, a Jewish physician and philosopher, recommended chicken soup to aid those suffering from colds and respiratory illnesses.

Healing chicken soups appear all over the globe. Mexicans flavor theirs with rice, lime, and hot peppers. The French flavor theirs with herbs and garlic. Germans enjoy chicken soup with spaetzle, Belgians with leeks, celery, and egg yolks, and the Chinese call for ginger, scallions, and star anise.

There's often deep-seated wisdom in traditional culinary folklore. Recently, researchers out of the University of Nebraska Medical Center have investigated the curative and restorative properties of chicken soup, discovering, scientifically, what your grandmother knew all along: chicken soup really is good for a cold.

Many of broth's constituent proteins like glutamine and glycine act as anti-inflammatories, and chicken broth in particular has been found to mitigate neutrophil migration; that is, it helps reduce the inflammatory response that makes you feel bad when you're suffering from a cold. Moreover, researchers have found that consuming chicken soup improves congestion. Chicken soup also helps the tiny hair-like structures in the nose and bronchial passages called cilia to function better and move more quickly, allowing them to protect against potential contagions.

So while chicken soup may not cure a cold precisely, it can certainly help you feel better, and there's scientific evidence to support this bit of traditional kitchen wisdom.

thai-style chicken soup with lemongrass and coconut milk (tom kha gai)

serves 6

4 cups Chicken Foot Stock (page 30)

½ pound shiitakes, thinly sliced, stems reserved

3 Thai chiles, smashed

1 (6-inch) stalk of lemongrass, smashed

1 (1-inch) knob ginger, peeled, skin reserved

6 makrut lime leaves, or 1 lime

2 shallots, peeled and diced, skins reserved

1½ pounds boneless, skinless chicken thighs, chopped into bite-size pieces

1 (13.5-ounce) can full-fat coconut milk

¼ cup fish sauce

1 tablespoon palm sugar

Cilantro sprigs, for garnish

Thai basil, for garnish

Lime wedges, for serving

I love Thai cooking, its passionate use of hot chiles and vibrant herbs and the interplay of sweet, sour, and salty flavors in each dish. Each of those notes come into play in this chicken soup, perfumed with fragrant lemongrass and lime leaf, spiked with Thai chiles and dotted with shiitakes and bites of flavorsome chicken thighs. Full-fat coconut milk smoothes out the bite of the chiles while fish sauce provides the salt that rounds out the flavor of the soup. I like to serve the soup accompanied by a bowlful of steamed rice, followed by sliced mango dressed with a squeeze of lime for dessert.

....

Pour the stock into a large saucepan and bring it to a simmer over medium heat. Toss the shiitake stems, chiles, lemongrass, ginger peelings, shallot skins, and lime leaves into the simmering broth. Cover the saucepan, and let the broth infuse with the aromas and flavors for about 20 minutes.

Turn off the heat and strain the broth it into a pitcher or jar through a fine-mesh sieve, discarding the solids. Wipe the saucepan clean with a kitchen towel to remove any stray debris.

Return the flavored broth to the saucepan and then add mushroom caps, sliced ginger, and shallots. Spoon in the chopped chicken thighs. Stir the coconut milk, fish sauce, and palm sugar into the broth and simmer over medium heat until the vegetables soften and the chicken cooks through, turning an opaque white, about 25 minutes.

Ladle into soup bowls, garnish with sprigs of cilantro and Thai basil, and serve with lime wedges alongside.

why you should choose pastured poultry

If you head to a farmers' market or farm stand and happen to find someone selling pasture-raised chickens or turkeys there, snatch them up while you can. Many farmers who raise their animals outdoors process them only two or three times a year, and may not be able to offer you a steady supply, so it's worth picking up one for that night's dinner and a few extra to freeze because they make the best-tasting and most flavorful broth.

When an animal is given room to roam and move about as its natural instincts compel it to do, the components that build flavor are able to more readily accumulate in its meat. The more an animal moves its muscles, the greater the need for those muscles to receive oxygen, and the more those muscles produce myoglobin protein, an oxygen-carrying protein that is high in iron. Myoglobin protein reacts with heat to create flavor, and as a result, the meat of pasture-raised animals is more flavorful than the meat of animals held in confinement, without the freedom to roam.

Pasture-raised poultry is also richer in micronutrients, owing to the varied diet of grubs, bugs, insects, sprouts, and supplemental feed they consume. Birds raised indoors eat feed comprised of corn, soy, rice bran, and wheat; they may even eat poultry feathers. The varied diet of pasture-raised birds means they consume more nutrients, and those nutrients work their way into their meat and fat, resulting in a favorable ratio of omega-3 to omega-6 fatty acids, as well as a higher levels of vitamin E, vitamin A, and beta carotene in their meat, fat, and eggs.

When these birds are allowed to enjoy their natural diet, and their natural rhythms of movement outdoors, they produce not only more flavorful meat, but meat that offers better nourishment than those of their confined peers.

turkey soup with root vegetables and wild rice

serves 6

1 cup wild rice

1 tablespoon apple cider vinegar

1 tablespoon butter

1 yellow onion, diced

2 cloves garlic, finely chopped

3 carrots, diced

2 parsnips, diced

1 celeriac, diced

1 tablespoon fresh thyme leaves

½ teaspoon finely ground sea salt

2 cups chopped, cooked turkey

6 cups Roasted Turkey Bone Broth (page 33)

Freshly ground black pepper

Whenever we have leftover turkey, I like to make this soup. The caramelized notes of roasted turkey balance nicely with the wild rice's nuttiness and the sweet and earthy notes of carrots, parsnips, and celeriac. Native to North America, wild rice grows in shallow lakes and ponds. It is particularly rich in B vitamins, as well as the minerals zinc, phosphorus, and manganese. Soaking the wild rice in water with a touch of vinegar shortens its cooking time while reducing food phytate, a component of grains and seeds that can inhibit the absorption of the minerals they contain.

Pour the rice into a mixing bowl, cover with warm water by 1 inch, and stir in the vinegar. Cover the bowl loosely with a kitchen towel to prevent stray debris from falling in. Let the rice soak overnight, at least 8 and up to 24 hours, then drain it, discarding the water.

Melt the butter in a heavy soup pot over medium heat. When the butter begins to foam and froth, turn the temperature down to medium-low and toss in the onion, garlic, carrots, parsnips, celeriac, and thyme. Sprinkle the salt over the vegetables and cover the pot, allowing the vegetables to sweat, undisturbed, until tender, about 10 minutes.

Give the vegetables one quick stir and then add the cooked turkey and soaked wild rice. Pour in the broth and simmer, covered, until the rice is tender, about 45 minutes.

Season with salt and pepper and serve warm.

stewing hens make the best broth

While any whole chicken will do in making broth, a stewing hen will give you superb results.

As animals age, two things happen to their meat: It grows richer in flavor and it toughens. The chickens sold as fryers, broilers, or roasting birds at farmer's markets and in grocery stores are young birds, culled at an early age of about six to eight weeks. These young birds give tender meat.

Laying or stewing hens, by contrast, are culled at an older age. Unlike frying and roasting birds, these chickens are bred lean and hearty and for egg production. As these birds age, they lay eggs with less frequency until they stop laying eggs altogether at around eight years old.

While these hens are not suitable for roasting and frying, they are perfect for the soup pot. Their meat is tougher and more flavorful than that of chickens bred for meat production, and they also accumulate a fair amount of rich yellow fat. As you simmer the hen, that fat renders, and will rise to the surface of any broth. Spoon this fat off and use it as a cooking fat; it has a delicious flavor and lovely texture owing to its high content of monounsaturated fat.

Stewing hens are not only perfect for making stocks and long-simmered bone broths like Whole Chicken Broth (page 28), but are also excellent in dishes that make their own broth like Cream of Chicken Soup with Parsley and Chives (page 78) and Yucatán-Style Lime Soup (page 81).

You can usually find stewing hens at farmers markets and farm stands, or ask your egg provider to save you a hen the next time she culls her flock. It's well worth it.

cream of chicken soup with parsley and chives

serves 8

6 celery stalks, including leaves

3 carrots, including the carrot tops

1 yellow onion

1 whole stewing hen (3 to 4 pounds)

2 leeks, cleaned

3 whole cloves

2 tablespoons butter

¼ teaspoon freshly grated nutmeg

6 egg yolks, beaten

2 cups heavy cream

2 tablespoons chopped flat-leaf parsley

2 tablespoons chopped chives

Growing up, all I knew of creamed soups is that they came from a red-and-white can that, when opened, would yield a bouncy gelatinous goop that served as the glue that bound the casseroles we would take to church potlucks. This soup is not one of those; rather, it's a lovely, comforting blend of aromatic vegetables, butter, egg yolks, cream, fresh herbs, and chicken.

This soup makes little waste, and in a home where every penny counts, it's rather nice to eke out every bit of flavor and nourishment from what you have available to you. So, use up the celery leaves and the carrot tops, and you'll find they give the soup a beautiful aromatic flavor that blends well with the soft and soothing flavor of chicken, cream, parsley and chives. This soup may separate when stored, so it's best eaten right away. Adapted from James Beard's *Fireside Cookbook*.

....

Pluck the leaves from the celery and place them in a stockpot. Chop off the carrot tops and peel the carrots, dropping both the peelings and tops into the pot. Chop off the root and top ends of the onion and then peel it, tucking the onion trimmings into the pot. Mince the celery, carrots, and onions very finely and then place them in a mixing bowl.

Rinse the chicken thoroughly and pat dry before adding it to the stockpot, covering it completely with cold water by about 2 inches.

Pierce the leek with the cloves so that they remain stuck inside its tender stalk and place it in the stockpot alongside the stewing chicken.

Slowly simmer until the chicken is completely cooked and tender to the bone, about 2 hours. Carefully remove the chicken from the pot and place it on a platter to allow it to cool until you can pick the meat off the bones comfortably.

continued

Strain the remaining broth through a fine-mesh sieve, into a pitcher or jar, discarding the solids. Wipe the pot clean with a kitchen towel.

Melt the butter in a cast-iron skillet until it foams, toss the minced vegetables and fry until they become fragrant and tender, about 5 minutes. Transfer to a clean stock pot.

Once the chicken has cooled, pick its meat off the bones (reserve the bones for Double-Cooked Stock, page 48). Mince the meat very finely. Stir the chicken into the vegetables and pour the strained broth back into the stock pot. Stir in the finely grated nutmeg, and then bring it all to a bare simmer over medium heat.

Temper the beaten eggs by stirring a spoonful of broth into the eggs, then pouring the mixture of eggs and broth into the simmering soup. Gently stir in the heavy cream, parsley, and chives. Season with salt and pepper.

Ladle into soup bowls and serve warm.

yucatán-style lime soup
(sopa de lima)

serves 8

Lard or coconut oil, for frying

1 (8-ounce) package corn tortillas, sliced into ¼ by 1-inch strips

1 whole chicken, about 3 pounds

1 white onion, thinly sliced

1 cup long-grain white rice

3 limes

Jalapeños, for garnish

Cotija cheese, for garnish

Cilantro sprigs, for garnish

1 avocado, sliced, for garnish

On a visit to Mexico's Yucatàn Peninsula, a place that offers a unique, lively cuisine steeped in both Mayan and Spanish culinary influence, my family climbed the vine-draped limestone ruins at Cobá, before our guide drove us along the winding orange-red roads through the jungle. We reached a *cenote*, a deep, naturally occurring limestone well filled with clean fresh water, where we swam until tired and worn. Now hungry from climbing and swimming, we headed to a small restaurant along the lake at Cobá, where they served traditional Yucatecan cooking. Among the dishes they offered was a classic lime soup. Nearly every restaurant along the Yucatán Peninsula offers its own perfect version of lime soup, some with bell peppers and others touched with cinnamon and oregano. I favor the simplest approach with chicken, onion, rice, and limes. Simple foods often make the best foods, as their humble ingredients shine through without pomp or pretense.

....

Line a plate with a paper towel or a cotton kitchen towel.

Set a cast-iron skillet over medium heat. Spoon enough lard into the skillet so that when it melts, it reaches about ½ inch up the side of the skillet, about 1½ cups.

Once the fat melts completely and begins to shimmer in the skillet, test the oil by dropping a tortilla strip into the hot fat. If the tortilla sizzles immediately in the pan, crisping and turning a golden brown within about 30 seconds, the oil is ready. Working in batches, and taking care not to crowd the pan, fry the tortilla strips until crisp and golden brown. Using a slotted spoon, transfer the tortilla strips to the lined plate, and allow them to cool. Turn off the heat.

continued

Place the whole chicken in a large stock pot. Pour enough water into the pot to cover the chicken by 2 inches. Bring the pot to a boil over medium-high heat, then immediately reduce the heat to medium-low and simmer, covered, for 2 hours, or until the chicken is cooked through and the meat shreds easily with a fork. Turn off the heat.

Carefully remove the chicken from the pot, setting it on a platter to allow it to cool until it's comfortable enough to handle. Remove and discard the skin, pull the meat from the bone, and shred it with a fork.

Strain the broth in the pot through a fine-mesh sieve into a pitcher or jar, discarding the solids. Wipe out the pot to remove any stray debris, and then return the strained broth and reserved chicken meat to the pot. Stir in the onion and rice and then bring to a simmer over medium heat. While the soup warms, juice one of the limes and then stir the juice into the soup pot. Continue cooking until the onion is soft and translucent, the rice is tender, and the chicken is warmed. While soup is cooking, finely chop the remaining 2 limes, peel and all.

Ladle into soup bowls and serve with the chopped lime, sliced jalapeño, crumbled Cotija cheese, sliced avocado, and tortilla strips.

chicken in wine with mushrooms, peas, and herbs

serves 6

2 tablespoons butter

1 whole chicken, about
4 pounds, cut into pieces

2 leeks, thinly sliced

1 pound button mushrooms,
thinly sliced

1 teaspoon finely ground
sea salt

2 cups dry white wine

1 1/2 pounds English peas
in their shell, or 2 cups
frozen peas

1 bunch flat-leaf parsley,
finely chopped

1 bunch chives, finely
chopped

1/2 cup crème fraîche

Spring arrives in my garden in a fit of sweet English peas, ready for shelling, and aromatic herbs. They marry well together, balanced by cream and mild-flavored button mushrooms. This dish, decidedly one of my favorites, is one I find myself making again and again. Elegant enough for company, but simple enough for a weeknight family dinner, it starts by browning chicken and then simmering it with wine, leeks, mushrooms, and peas until the meat falls off the bone. The broth, enhanced with crème fraîche, makes a lovely sauce, and I serve this over potatoes.

....

Warm the butter in the bottom of a Dutch oven over medium heat. Working in batches to prevent overcrowding, add the chicken pieces to the pot and brown them, about 6 minutes on each side. Remove the chicken from the pan and stir then stir in the leeks and mushrooms. Add the salt to the pot, cover it, and turn down the heat to medium-low. Allow the leeks and mushrooms to sweat together in the heat of the pot until tender, about 8 minutes. Return the chicken to the pot and then pour in the white wine. Simmer it all together over medium-low heat until the chicken is tender, about 45 minutes.

If you're using fresh peas still in their shell, shell them while the chicken cooks. Pour them into the pan and then continue simmering them all together until the peas soften and become tender, a further 20 minutes.

If you're using frozen peas, continue cooking the chicken another 15 minutes and then pour in the peas, allowing them to warm, about 5 minutes more. Stir the parsley and chives into the pot. Turn off the heat, stir in the crème fraîche, season with sea salt, and serve hot.

dashi-braised chicken thighs

serves 6

2 cups Dashi (page 39)

1 pound shiitakes, stems reserved and caps sliced ¼ inch thick

2 tablespoons coconut oil

1 clove garlic

1 (1-inch) knob ginger

6 skinless, bone-in chicken thighs

2 tablespoons mirin

6 green onions, white, light green, and dark green parts, sliced thinly on the diagonal

1 tablespoon sesame seeds

Steamed rice, for serving

From time to time, my family sits down to a dinner of these chicken thighs, slowly braised in dashi, sprinkled with green onions and sesame seeds and served with bowls of steamed rice and vegetables. Chicken thighs benefit from the long, slow process of braising that cooks them to a nearly impossible tenderness, making their meat fall off the bone.

Rather than using chicken stock or broth, I favor using dashi, which like all broths and stocks, makes a wonderful braising liquid, and its umami-rich flavor is well complemented by sesame seeds, ginger, and garlic.

. . . .

Warm the dashi in a small saucepan over medium heat. Drop the shiitake stems into the saucepan so that they impart their flavor to the broth as it heats. After 10 minutes, strain the broth and discard the mushroom stems. Keep the broth warm while you prepare the other ingredients.

Melt the coconut oil in a wide skillet over medium heat. When the oil begins to shimmer in the skillet, drop in the garlic and ginger, sautéing them together until they release their aroma, about 3 minutes. Arrange the chicken in the skillet and brown each piece in the hot fat, about 5 minutes per side.

Using a pair of tongs, remove each piece of chicken from the pan and set it on a plate. Stir in the sliced shiitake caps and sauté them until cooked through and fragrant, about 8 minutes.

Turn down the heat to medium-low and return the chicken to the pan. Pour in the dashi and mirin. Cover the pan and simmer the ingredients together for 10 minutes, then remove the cover, turn the heat up to medium-high, and continue braising the chicken until cooked through and tender, a further 10 to 15 minutes or so. Sprinkle the cooked chicken and mushrooms with the sliced onions and sesame seeds.

Serve warm in bowls over steamed rice.

meat

Where poultry stock and broth is light and versatile, beef and pork broths and stocks are robust and striking. Their rich notes need equally full-bodied spices and vegetables to give them balance and provide a hearty base for the meat dishes included in this chapter. Beef and pork stocks and broths provide ample protein but a relatively modest amount of minerals. That mineral content can be improved by the inclusion of vegetables. You might sip these savory stocks and broths on their own, or use them as the base for light soups, to fortify stews or in pan sauces.

Ranchers typically process their steers and hogs in autumn or early winter. For this reason, I tend to lean more heavily on these richer and more hardy stocks and broths in the colder months of winter during which time their strong flavor is both welcome and intuitively satisfying.

beef tea

makes 4 cups

1 pound round steak, finely chopped

Finely ground salt

Freshly ground black pepper

4 cups cold water

In the nineteenth century, home cooks prepared a broth they called beef tea to nourish ill and convalescent family members. They began first by packing a jar with chopped meat, filling it with water, sealing it, and simmering it in hopes of extracting the goodness of meat into the broth. Its flavor is rich, strong, and decidedly meaty, and it is excellent served with a sprinkle of salt. You don't need to reserve it for times of illness, as nineteenth-century home cooks did; rather, you can enjoy it as sipping broth any time that strikes your fancy.

....

Drop the meat into a 1-quart jar. Cover the chopped meat with cold water by 1-inch (about 4 cups) and then seal the lid on the jar tightly. Place a canning rack in a stockpot and set the jar on the rack. Pour enough water into the stockpot to reach the shoulders of the jar. Bring to a slow boil over medium-high heat and then lower the heat to medium. Simmer for 4 hours, then remove the jar from the pot and allow it to cool until it's comfortable to handle.

Strain the liquid through a fine-mesh sieve into another 1-quart jar, discarding the solids. Seal the jar tightly and set it in the refrigerator where it will keep for up to 1 week.

To serve, spoon off any hardened fat and then warm the beef tea in a saucepan on the stove. Season with salt and pepper and serve warm.

portable soup

makes about 24 nuggets, for 12 quarts of soup

2 veal knuckles

2 beef shins

3 yellow onions, halved lengthwise, unpeeled and untrimmed

1 small bunch thyme

1 tablespoon whole black peppercorns

1 teaspoon freshly grated nutmeg

6 whole cloves

Before home cooks could stop by the store to pick up little boxes of foil-wrapped powdery cubes of bouillon, there was portable soup. Once made, these nuggets of preserved broth provided easy sustenance for travel. Cooks simmered vast quantities of beef bones in giant cauldrons down to a thick, gelatinous, ropy syrup that they later dried into glassy nuggets for storage. I make my own version of portable soup, using a smaller quantity of bones, that simmer and reduce down to form gelatin-rich cubes of stock that store easily in the fridge and reconstitute instantly into stock when dropped into hot water.

....

Place the veal knuckles and beef shins into a large, heavy stockpot and cover with water by 1 inch. Drop the onions into the pot. Stir in the thyme, peppercorns, nutmeg, and cloves. Bring it all to a boil over medium-high heat, and then immediately turn down the temperature to medium-low. Simmer, covered, for 12 hours, or until any meat softens and easily separates from bones. Skim away any scum that foams up at the surface of the broth while it boils.

Strain the broth through a fine-mesh sieve into a large jar, discarding the solids. Seal the jar tightly, and then let it sit in the refrigerator overnight or until the fat hardens.

Scoop away the fat that hardens on the surface of the broth, and then pour the broth into a double boiler set over medium-high heat. Continue cooking the broth until reduced to one-tenth of its original volume, forming a thick and ropy syrup.

Pour the broth into ice cube trays, and then transfer the trays to the refrigerator to allow the reduced broth to gel, about 12 hours.

Remove the gelled broth from the trays and store them in an airtight container in the refrigerator for 6 weeks or in the freezer for 6 months.

To serve the broth, pluck a nugget of portable soup from the container and dissolve it in 2 cups boiling water. Adjust the seasoning and add vegetables as it suits you.

quick pho

serves 4

1½ pounds top sirloin

1 yellow onion, halved

1 (3-inch) knob fresh ginger, halved

2 pods star anise

1 cinnamon stick, about 3 inches long

1 teaspoon whole coriander seeds

½ teaspoon fennel seeds

2 whole cloves

2 quarts Long-Simmered Roasted Beef Bone Broth (page 34)

¼ cup fish sauce

1 (8-ounce) package dried Vietnamese-style flat rice noodles

4 green onions, cut on the diagonal into 1-inch-wide slices

1 bunch cilantro

1 bunch Thai basil

1 bunch mint

2 limes, quartered lengthwise

2 jalapeños, thinly sliced

¼ cup hoisin sauce

¼ cup Sriracha sauce

Popularized in the West after the Vietnam War, pho is a classic Vietnamese soup of spiced broth, rice noodles, herbs, and thinly sliced meat.

Pho is blessedly easy to make at home, as long you happen to have some beef stock on hand, and it comes together for a nice and quick weeknight meal. You can prepare pho's classic accompaniments of hot peppers, fresh herbs, bean sprouts, and lime while the beef stock warms on your stove, and takes on the characteristic flavors of coriander, fennel, cinnamon, and cloves.

....

Place the meat in the freezer, this will make the meat easier to slice thinly.

Drop the yellow onion and ginger along with the star anise, cinnamon, coriander, fennel seeds, and cloves into a 4-quart pot and then pour the broth over the vegetables and spices. Add the fish sauce and bring it all to a simmer over medium-high heat.

While the broth simmers, set the rice noodles in a deep mixing bowl and cover them with boiling water. Leave them in the hot water until tender but not mushy, about 10 minutes. When tender, drain them in a colander.

While the rice noodles soak in the hot water and the broth simmers, arrange the green onions on a serving platter. Separate the leaves of cilantro, Thai basil, and mint from their stems. Arrange the herbs and bean sprouts, as well as the limes and jalapeños, on the serving platter alongside the green onions.

continued

quick pho, continued

Take the meat from the freezer, and then slice it against the grain into wafer-thin pieces. Arrange the sliced meat in a small bowl. Spoon the hoisin sauce and Sriracha sauce into separate bowls.

Arrange about one-quarter of the noodles into a nest in each of four individual bowls and then strain about 1½ cups broth over the noodles into each bowl, taking care that no spices from the simmering broth make their way into the bowls.

Serve the bowls of steaming-hot noodle soup. Encourage everyone at the table to add herbs, peppers, meat, and hoisin sauce, individualizing the seasonings and additions in their bowl as it suits them.

beef consommé with chives,
and mushrooms

serves 6

8 ounces button mushrooms, caps and stems separated and thinly sliced

1 leek, white and light green parts thinly sliced

3 celery salks, finely chopped

1 clove garlic, finely chopped

4 egg whites

6 cups Long-Simmered Roasted Beef Bone Broth (page 34)

Finely ground sea salt

2 tablespoons chopped fresh chives

Thinly sliced mushroom caps and a sprinkling of fresh herbs add another dimension to this classic beef consommé, which serves as a beautiful start to a more substantial meal. Consommé is traditionally a light, unsubstantial soup, and its star is a perfectly clear stock.

. . . .

In a large mixing bowl, drop in the thinly sliced mushroom stems along with the leek, celery, and garlic.

In a separate bowl, whisk the egg whites together until foamy and then fold them into the finely chopped vegetables until well combined.

Pour the broth into a stock pot and then stir in the egg white mixture. Warm the pot over medium-high heat, stirring continuously, until the broth begins to simmer. Turn down the heat to medium-low and stop stirring. The egg whites and vegetables will rise to the surface of the stock and begin to form a raft. Continue to keep broth at a bare simmer, undisturbed, for 30 minutes, and then turn off the heat.

While the broth simmers, arrange the thinly sliced mushroom caps in a soup tureen or serving dish.

Once the stock is clear, gently press the raft of egg whites down with a ladle until the ladle begins to fill with clarified broth, then pour this through a fine-mesh sieve over the mushroom caps. Continue until all that remains in the stockpot is the egg white raft. Discard the raft.

Season the consommé with salt as it suits you, and then sprinkle in the chives. Serve warm.

beef stew with winter vegetables

serves 6

2 tablespoons all-purpose flour

2 teaspoons finely ground sea salt

2 teaspoons finely ground black pepper

2 pounds beef stew meat

3 cups Long-Simmered Roasted Beef Bone Broth with its hardened cap of fat (page 34)

3 yellow onions, peeled and quartered

2 carrots, chopped

2 parsnips, chopped

1 celeriac, chopped

3 russet potatoes, chopped

¼ cup tomato paste

1 cup dry red wine

2 bay leaves

In late autumn, my family visits local farms, and I order hearty root vegetables by the case: dark red and muted yellow beets, purple-topped turnips, gnarled and knotted celeriac, carrots, and parsnips, as well as loads of potatoes with the soil still clinging to them. These starchy roots sustain us in the colder months when we look for something comforting and substantial.

As the winter days grow colder and darker, my family craves hearty meals—long-simmered soups and robust stews like this one. It's a beautiful combination: earthy root vegetables paired with fresh beef, seasoned simply with salt and pepper, red wine, and sweet bay leaves.

Keep in mind that if you avoid gluten by necessity or choice, both arrowroot powder and white rice flour work fine as a substitute for all-purpose flour, performing the function of thickening the stew as it simmers.

....

Preheat the oven to 325°F.

Spoon the flour, salt, and pepper into a small bowl and whisk them together until just combined. Sprinkle the seasoned flour over the stew meat, tossing them gently together until the flour lightly coats the meat.

Spoon 2 tablespoons of the hardened fat from the top of the jar of broth and drop it into a Dutch oven set over medium-high heat. When the fat melts, toss in the stew meat, browning it on all sides, about 8 minutes.

Once the meat browns, tuck all of the vegetables into the Dutch oven alongside it. In a separate bowl, stir the tomato paste into the wine until loosely combined, and then pour it all over the meat and vegetables. Pour in the broth and drop in the bay leaves then bake, covered, about 3 hours, or until the meat is fork-tender. Serve immediately, sprinkled with salt and freshly ground pepper, or store in the fridge overnight to allow its flavors to marry before reheating it on the stove top until warm.

black bean soup

serves 6 to 8

1½ cups dried black beans, picked over and rinsed well

¼ teaspoon baking soda

2 tablespoons coconut oil

1 white onion, quartered

3 cloves garlic, minced

2 teaspoons ground cumin

1 teaspoon chile powder

1 teaspoon dried oregano

4 cups Long-Simmered Roasted Beef Bone Broth (page 34)

1 (28-ounce) can diced tomatoes

Sour cream, for serving

Minced red onion, for serving

Cilantro sprigs, for serving

Sliced jalapeño, for serving

In late autumn and early December, when the weather turns a touch colder, our Community Supported Agriculture (CSA) farmer packs little bags full of beans she's grown, dried, and cleaned, into our farmshare box. I transfer these to jars in my cupboards where they keep well until the next year's harvest is ready.

Earthy and mild in flavor, beans pair well with more assertive companions, and in one of our favorite soups, garlic, cumin, and chile round out the beans' flavor. I ladle the soup into bowls, and we spike each one with a dollop of sour cream, a sprinkling of minced red onion or fresh cilantro leaves, and a few slices of jalapeño. Just like chili, this soup gains flavor over time and can be even more delicious the next day, though it might thicken overnight, so pour a bit of water or leftover broth into the pot before you warm the soup and serve it again.

....

Dump the beans into a mixing bowl, cover them with warm water by 2 inches, and then stir in the baking soda. Place a lid over the bowl, or drape it with a kitchen towel to keep out dust, and then allow the beans to soak for at least 18 and up to 24 hours. After they've soaked, drain them through a fine-mesh sieve and rinse them well. Leave the soaked beans in a mixing bowl on your countertop while you prepare the other ingredients.

Warm the coconut oil in a heavy stock pot over medium-high heat and then stir in the onion and garlic, sautéing them in the hot fat until they release their aroma and begin to color, just a touch, at their edges, about 8 minutes. Stir the cumin, chile powder, and oregano into the onions and garlic until just combined.

continued

Add the soaked beans to the pot and then pour in the broth and the diced tomatoes. Turn down the heat to medium-low and simmer, covered, stirring occasionally, for 2½ hours, or until the beans are tender and soft enough to yield without resistance when pressed down with the back of a spoon.

Puree the bean-broth with an immersion blender to break up about half of the beans, forming a creamy broth. If you don't have an immersion blender, or prefer a chunkier texture to your soup, skip this step and serve it as is.

Ladle the soup into bowls and serve warm with sour cream, minced red onion, cilantro, and sliced jalapeño.

salisbury steak with mushroom sauce

serves 4

1 pound ground beef

2 shallots, minced

1 egg yolk

1 teaspoon unrefined sea salt

½ teaspoon freshly ground black pepper

2 cups Long-Simmered Roasted Beef Bone Broth with its hardened cap of fat (page 34)

2 cups dry red wine

2 sprigs thyme

2 tablespoons butter (plus more if needed)

1 large yellow onion, halved and thinly sliced

1 pound mushrooms, thinly sliced

I remember Salisbury steak from the lunch lines at my elementary school, where it was served slopped on a bright orange melamine tray. Now that we buy a steer from a local rancher every autumn, I'm left with piles of beef bones and plenty of ground meat. Salisbury steak, smothered in mushroom and onion sauce and served with a pile of mashed potatoes, makes its appearance on our table often, particularly during winter months when we yearn for something hearty. Of course this isn't the stuff of TV dinners and elementary-school lunch lines; rather, it's rich with the bright flavor of minced shallots, robust wine, and earthy mushrooms.

....

In a large mixing bowl, knead the ground beef and minced shallots together to coarsely combine them. Using a wooden spoon, beat in the egg yolk, salt, and pepper until thoroughly combined.

Form the seasoned meat into four patties and set them on a waiting plate while you begin preparing the mushroom and onion reduction sauce.

Spoon 4 tablespoons of fat from the cap that naturally seals the broth. If the cap doesn't yield a full 4 tablespoons you can supplement it with butter. Pour the broth and red wine into a saucepan and bring it to a boil over high heat. Drop in the thyme and continue boiling it until you've reduced the broth by three-quarters.

Melt 2 tablespoons of butter in a cast-iron or stainless steel skillet over a medium-high heat. Toss in the onion slices and sauté them until they release their fragrance and their edges begin to caramelize. Remove the onions from the pan to a bowl. Add the mushrooms to the pan and sauté until they are fragrant and brown. Spoon the mushrooms into the bowl with the cooked onions.

continued

Melt 2 tablespoons more of the reserved fat in the skillet and add the beef patties to the hot fat, searing on both sides until nice and brown on the outside but still pink in the center. Smother them with the mushrooms and onions.

Once the wine and broth have reduced, remove and discard the sprigs of thyme. Pour the reduction sauce over the Salisbury steaks, mushrooms, and onions. Continue to simmer over a moderately low flame until the steaks are cooked through, about 3 to 4 minutes further.

Serve hot, with the pan sauce.

galician pork and bean stew with greens (caldo gallego)

serves 8

1 cup dried white beans, such as cannellini or great Northern beans, picked over and rinsed well

¼ teaspoon baking soda

2 tablespoons extra-virgin olive oil

4 cloves garlic, minced

1 yellow onion, peeled chopped

1 smoked ham hock, about 1 pound

2 bay leaves

8 cups water

8 ounces Spanish chorizo, sliced into rounds ¼ inch thick

1 pound potatoes, peeled and chopped into 1-inch cubes

1 pound turnips, peeled and chopped into ½-inch cubes, greens reserved

Finely ground sea salt

Olive oil, for drizzling (optional)

Heavy with earthy white beans and sturdy root vegetables, *caldo gallego* is a brothy stew originating from the rocky hills and mountains of northern Spain. Cured pork and starchy root vegetables, both prominent aspects of Galicia's traditional food pathways, serve to stay the region's population against cold winters.

Like many regional dishes, *caldo gallego* varies in its exact ingredients from house to house, garden to garden, and season to season, though pork, white beans, roots, and greens always make an appearance. A friend who lived with her extended family in rural Galicia during her childhood described to me the tradition of serving this stew: First, the broth is strained from the solids and served alone as an appetizer to whet the palate for the meat, beans, and vegetables, which are served later, as you might do with a pot roast.

Whether you serve the soup in courses or, as is more common today, in one hearty bowl, you'll find this to be a satisfying and deeply nourishing supper.

. . . .

Dump the beans into a mixing bowl and pour enough water into the bowl to cover the beans by 1 inch. Stir in the baking soda, cover the bowl loosely with a kitchen towel, and let the beans soak for at least 8 and up to 24 hours. Drain them and rinse well.

Warm the olive oil in a Dutch oven over medium-high heat. Toss in the garlic and onion, sautéing in the hot oil until they release their aroma, about 6 minutes. Add the ham hock to the pot, searing on each side.

continued

Turn the heat down to medium-low. Dump the soaked beans into the pot and then drop in the bay leaves. Pour in the water, cover the pot, and let it simmer for 2 hours, or until the meat easily pulls away from the bone and the beans are tender.

Once the ham hock and beans simmer into a lovely, rich broth, drop in the chorizo and potatoes. Continue stewing the meats, beans, and potatoes together for 20 minutes more, or until tender.

Drop the turnip cubes into the pot. Set the reserved turnip greens on your cutting board. Trim off any tough stems and discard them and then chop the remaining greens coarsely. Stir the greens into the stew and continue cooking, covered, 5 to 10 minutes more, or until the greens are tender.

Turn off the heat. Remove the ham hock from the pot with a pair of tongs. Pull off and shred any meat that adheres to the bone with a fork. Return the meat to the pot and discard the bone. Season the stew with salt to taste.

Ladle the soup into bowls and serve warm, with additional olive oil sprinkled on top.

oxtail stew

serves 6

1½ cups dry white beans, picked over for debris and rinsed

¼ teaspoon baking soda

4 pounds oxtails

1 teaspoon sea salt

½ teaspoon ground black pepper

2 tablespoons extra virgin olive oil

8 ounces bacon, finely chopped

3 cloves garlic, minced

4 celery ribs, diced

3 carrots, peeled and diced

¼ cup tomato paste

2 cups red wine

2 (14.5-ounce) cans peeled and diced tomatoes

2 bay leaves

1 dozen pearl onions, peeled

Oxtail is an inexpensive cut of beef that produces a richly flavored, gelatinous stock. Its natural, strong meatiness overpowers subtle and light flavors, and it needs a partner robust enough to contend with its assertiveness. Tomatoes, garlic, bacon, and onion do the trick here for a classic oxtail stew. The inclusion of white beans gives the stew a starchiness required to make it a substantial and inexpensive meal.

....

Pour the rinsed beans into a mixing bowl, cover them with warm water by 2 inches, and stir in the baking soda. Cover the bowl with a tight-fitting lid or a lint-free kitchen towel and allow them to soak, undisturbed, for at least 12 and up to 18 hours.

Drain the beans in a colander and rinse well.

Sprinkle the oxtails with salt and pepper and set on a plate to rest while you prepare the other additions to the soup pot.

Warm the olive oil in a Dutch oven set over medium heat. Working in batches, brown the oxtails, about 4 minutes on each side, and then transfer to a plate to rest.

Toss the bacon into the pan and let it cook in the hot fat until crisp, about 8 minutes. Stir in the garlic, celery, and carrots, sautéing them until fragrant, about 6 minutes. Return the oxtails to the pan and stir in the tomato paste, red wine, and tomatoes. Drop in the bay leaves and simmer, covered, for 3 hours, or until the oxtails are tender and the meat easily separates from the bones. Stir in the pearl onions, and soaked beans and continue simmering, covered, for 30 to 45 minutes further or until the beans are tender.

Pluck out the bay leaves, adjust seasoning with sea salt, and then ladle into soup bowls.

beef shank with garlic and basil

serves 6

2 tablespoons olive oil

4 pounds beef shanks

4 heads garlic, cloves removed, peeled, and crushed

1 yellow onion, peeled and chopped fine

3 celery stalks, diced

3 carrots, peeled and diced

Juice and finely grated zest of 1 orange

2 bay leaves

3 cups water

1 cup finely sliced basil leaves

Like most inexpensive cuts, beef shank is impossibly tough but flavorful, and stewing slowly tenderizes it, producing a flavor-forward broth with meat that falls off the bone. Olive oil, garlic, and basil seem like a natural pairing, while fresh orange offers an elusive but complex addition to the pot. This stew stores well, deepening in flavor when left to sit in the fridge overnight, and reheats easily. Keep it up to three days in the fridge or up to one month in the freezer.

. . . .

Preheat oven to 350°F.

Warm the olive oil in the bottom of a Dutch oven over medium heat. Brown the beef shanks, about 6 minutes on all sides. Remove the beef from the pan and add the garlic, onion, celery, and carrots. Sauté them together until fragrant, about 4 minutes.

Turn the heat down to medium-low, and then return the beef to the pan. Stir in the orange zest and the orange juice. Drop in the bay leaves and add the water.

Cover the pot, and bake the shanks in the oven until completely tender, about 3½ hours.

Pluck out the bay leaves, sprinkle with basil, and serve warm.

white bean and bacon soup

serves 8

2 cups navy beans, picked over for debris and rinsed

¼ teaspoon baking soda

1 teaspoon butter

8 ounces bacon, chopped into ¼-inch pieces

1 yellow onion, chopped into ¼-inch cubes

3 celery stalks, chopped

2 carrots, peeled and chopped

6 cups Long-Simmered Roasted Pork Bone Broth (page 36)

¼ cup tomato paste

Finely ground sea salt

I remember tucking into steaming bowls of White Bean and Bacon Soup as a kid, though then it came from a red-and-white can. I loved the way the beans fell apart, blending into a smooth, creamy broth dotted by salty, smoky bacon. Bacon and white beans make natural companions, as the rich smokiness of bacon proves a sure foil for beans' starchy leanness. This soup is also great served up with a sprinkling of crispy bacon on top as shown on the opposite page.

....

Pour the beans into a mixing bowl, cover with warm water by 2 inches, and then stir in the baking soda. Cover the bowl with a tight-fitting lid or with a kitchen towel to keep out stray dust and debris, and then allow the beans to soak at least 18 and up to 24 hours.

Drain the beans in a fine-mesh sieve or a colander and rinse the beans well.

Warm the butter in a heavy soup pot over medium-high heat. When it melts, drop in the chopped bacon, frying it in the hot fat until crisp, about 8 minutes.

Once the bacon has fried to a crisp, stir the onion, celery, and carrots into the pan and sauté them together with the bacon until they release their fragrance, about 6 minutes further.

Pour the soaked beans, the broth, and the tomato paste into the pot. Turn down the heat to medium-low and simmer, covered, stirring occasionally, for 1½ to 2 hours, or until the beans are tender and soft.

Puree the mixture with an immersion blender or food mill to break up about half of the beans, forming a creamy broth. Add enough salt to suit your taste, and then serve warm, ladled into soup bowls.

smoky black-eyed pea soup

serves 8

1 cup black-eyed peas, picked over and rinsed well

¼ teaspoon baking soda

2 tablespoons bacon fat

3 carrots, peeled and chopped

4 celery stalks, chopped

1 yellow onion, peeled and chopped

2 teaspoons smoked paprika

½ teaspoon cayenne pepper

6 cups Long-Simmered Roasted Pork Bone Broth (page 36)

Finely ground sea salt

1 bunch lacinto kale, coarsely chopped

Pork, black-eyed peas, and kale are natural companions. I serve this soup on New Year's, when folklore reminds us that pork, black-eyed peas, and leafy greens bring good fortune. When pigs are fortunate enough to root around outdoors, they move forward, symbolizing progress. Black-eyed peas traditionally represent coins. In this soup, they simmer together in a hearty broth made of roasted pork bones, seasoned with smoked paprika and a bright punch of cayenne pepper.

....

Dump the black-eyed peas into a mixing bowl and pour enough warm water into the bowl to cover the peas by 1 inch. Stir in the baking soda and allow them to soak at least 12 and up to 24 hours. Drain them in a fine-mesh sieve or a colander and rinse well.

Warm the bacon fat in a heavy soup pot over medium-high heat. Once completely melted, add the carrots, celery, and onion into the pot, sautéing them until fragrant, about 8 minutes. Stir in the paprika and cayenne and continue to cook for 2 minutes more. Stir in the broth and the soaked black-eyed peas. Turn down the heat to medium-low and simmer, covered, until the peas are tender, about 1 hour 10 minutes. Once the peas are tender, toss the kale into the pot, and simmer in the soup for 15 minutes further, or until completely wilted and tender. Adjust seasoning with salt, and serve warm.

pinto beans and ham hock

serves 8

3 cups dried pinto beans, picked over and rinsed

¼ teaspoon baking soda

1 tablespoon lard or bacon fat

1 white onion, peeled chopped

2 ham hocks, about 2 pounds

Finely ground sea salt

The most vivid memory I have of my grandmother's kitchen is of hurriedly eating sandwiches of white bread and margarine over the sink. Despite her lack of culinary prowess, my grandmother did make one dish and one dish very well: pinto beans and ham hock. Its simple ingredients and easy approach make it perfect for a novice cook or a harried one.

The combination of ham hock's natural sweet smokiness paired with the earthy and humble flavor of pinto beans make a satisfying, full-flavored meal.

. . . .

Pour the beans into a mixing bowl, cover with warm water by 2 inches, and stir in the baking soda. Soak for at least 8 and up to 18 hours, then drain and rinse them well.

Melt the lard in a heavy soup pot over medium heat. Stir the onion into the hot fat and sauté it until fragrant and translucent, about 8 minutes. Drop the ham hocks into the pot and then stir in the beans. Pour enough water into the pot to cover its contents by 2 inches and simmer, covered, over medium-low heat until the beans are soft and the meat falls away easily from the bone, about 3 hours.

Remove the ham hocks from the pot and, when they're cool enough to handle, pull any meat that still clings to it off the bone, and stir it into the pot of beans.

Season the beans with salt to taste, ladle into soup bowls, and serve hot.

pork pot roast with sweet potato, ancho chile, and lime

serves 6

Finely grated zest and juice of 2 limes, about 4 ounces each, plus additional limes for serving

2 teaspoons finely ground sea salt

1 teaspoon chili powder

1 teaspoon ground cumin

½ teaspoon ground chipotle chile

1 bone-in pork shoulder, about 4 pounds

1 tablespoon lard

2 cups beer

2 ancho chiles

2 white onions, peeled and quartered

8 cloves garlic, crushed

1 pound sweet potatoes, peeled and chopped into 1-inch cubes

Unlike fatty ham hocks or pork belly, a pork shoulder roast is a lean and meaty cut. As with other lean cuts, pork shoulder benefits from long, low, and slow cooking, producing lovely, fork-tender meat. This recipe calls for lard, a soft billowy white fat with a fatty acid profile similar to avocado and olive oil. When rendered from the fat of pasture-raised pigs, lard is also rich in vitamin D. You can spoon a bit of the fat you've reserved from making Long-Simmered Roasted Pork Bone Broth (page 36) to use in this recipe, or you can substitute olive oil.

....

In a small mixing bowl, stir lime zest, salt, chili powder, cumin, and ground chipotle together until uniformly combined. Sprinkle these seasonings over the pork shoulder on all sides.

Melt the lard in a Dutch oven over medium-high heat. Place the pork in the hot fat and sear it, about 3 minutes per side. Turn the heat down to medium-low, pour in the beer and ancho chiles, and let simmer, covered, for 3 hours, or until the meat easily pulls away from the bone when you pierce it with a fork.

Arrange the onions, garlic, and sweet potatoes around the meat in the Dutch oven. Cover the roast once more and then continue cooking for another 45 minutes or until the vegetables are tender.

Stir in the lime juice and serve warm, with wedges of fresh lime.

spicy chickpea and lamb stew

serves 6

1 cup dried chickpeas, picked over and rinsed well

¼ teaspoon baking soda

2 teaspoons ground cumin

2 teaspoons ground coriander

1 teaspoon powdered ginger

1 teaspoon ground fennel seed

1 teaspoon paprika

1 teaspoon turmeric

½ teaspoon freshly ground black pepper

½ teaspoon cayenne pepper

¼ teaspoon ground cinnamon

½ teaspoon ground allspice

1 teaspoon finely ground sea salt

2 lamb shanks, about 3 pounds

2 tablespoons extra-virgin olive oil

1 large yellow onion, peeled and sliced into eighths

4 carrots, peeled and chopped

2 large russet potatoes, peeled and chopped

1 cup dates, pitted and chopped

1 (14.5-ounce) can peeled and diced tomatoes

6 cups cold water

½ cup chopped fresh flat-leaf parsley leaves

I order a whole lamb each year from ranchers who keep their animals on pasture, which improves the quality of their meat. Ordering by the whole animal, rather than by the cut, keeps lamb affordable and my family well nourished, but it also leaves us with odd cuts like lamb shank. This recipe is inspired by the summer I spent in Morocco, where I learned how to prepare this lamb shank and chickpea stew. I like to serve this dish with a simple salad of cucumber and tomato, dressed with olive oil, lemon, and parsley.

....

Pour the rinsed chickpeas into a medium bowl, cover them with warm water by 2 inches, and stir in the baking soda. Cover the bowl with a kitchen towel and allow the chickpeas to soak for at least 12 and up to 18 hours. Drain them and rinse them well.

Whisk the spices and salt together in a small bowl, then sprinkle the mixture evenly over the lamb shanks.

Warm the olive oil in the bottom of a Dutch oven over high heat and then sear the seasoned lamb shanks on all sides, about 6 minutes per side.

Turn down the heat to medium-low and arrange the onion, carrots, potatoes, soaked chickpeas, dates, and tomatoes around the lamb. Pour in the water. Cover the pot and simmer until the lamb is tender enough to fall off the bone, about 2 hours.

Serve sprinkled with the chopped parsley leaves.

fish

My love of fish soup begins with chowder. In wintertime, I choose heavy cream chowders, but in summer I go for lighter varieties brimming with corn and shrimp and spiked with fresh jalapeño. Seaside communities enjoy traditional fish and shellfish soups of their own, often flavored with seaweeds. Among my favorites is miso soup, which comes together with a quick stir of miso paste into hot broth.

Fish and shellfish are delicate creatures, and they don't need or benefit from the extensive and prolonged cooking required for beef and chicken stocks; rather, seafood stocks come together quickly, needing less than an hour. Fish and shellfish stocks complement and enhance chowders and fish stews, reinforcing their light and delicate nature. Dashi, a traditional Japanese stock, by contrast, can give vegetables an elusive savory note.

finding good fish

With news of oceanic pollution perpetually increasing, choosing good-quality, clean, and sustainably caught fish and shellfish may seem like an insurmountable burden, and you might find yourself wondering if any of it is clean, if any waters are unpolluted, and if any fish live without threat of endangerment. However, all hope is not lost. Environmental stewardship and conservation taken in managing fisheries make some fish choices not only ecologically sustainable, but also deeply nourishing, as fish and shellfish are particularly rich in omega-3 fatty acids that help support cardiovascular, reproductive, emotional, and cognitive health, as well as vitamins and minerals like iron and selenium.

The smaller the fish, the less time there is for environmental pollutants like heavy metals to accumulate in their flesh, bones, and fat, making small, oily fish like sardines and anchovies particularly good choices. Similarly, salmon, sole, and mackerel tend to be low in heavy metal contamination.

Naturally plentiful stocks or well-managed fisheries are excellent resources for sustainable and non-threatened fish. Alaskan fisheries continue to be some of the most actively and intensively managed, making wild-caught Alaskan salmon, halibut, cod, and black cod particularly good choices. Farmed shellfish like oysters, clams, and mussels are also sustainable options and tend to be rich in trace minerals like iron as well as vitamin D, which helps support bone health, fertility, and immune system function.

The Monterey Bay Aquarium's Seafood Watch Program (seafoodwatch.org) is an excellent and up-to-date resource that monitors the relative sustainability of fish worldwide. The National Resources Defense Council (nrdc.org) provides an up-to-date list of the mercury content of various fish, rating them from low to high. Both resources help you make better choices for yourself, your family, and the environment when it comes to seafood.

pink shrimp chowder

serves 6

1 tablespoon butter

4 ounces bacon, chopped into ¼-inch pieces

1 yellow onion, peeled and chopped into ¼-inch dice

4 celery stalks, chopped into ¼-inch dice

¾ pound red potatoes, peeled and chopped into ¼-inch pieces

3 cups Fish Stock (page 37) or Shellfish Stock (page 40)

2 bay leaves

2 ears fresh sweet corn, kernels removed and cobs reserved

1 jalapeño, seeds removed, and sliced thin

¾ pound frozen Oregon pink shrimp

1 cup heavy cream

Pink shrimp are tiny crustaceans, about ½ an inch at their largest. Fishermen catch them by midwater trawling equipped with bycatch reduction devices in Washington and Oregon, a method that reduces damage to the ocean floor caused by other methods of trawling. Equipped with nets that allow other species to go free, this method of catching pink shrimp make these little creatures a sustainable choice. Pink shrimp are so charmingly little that you get a great many of them with every spoonful of chowder. Their sweet, briny flavor finds a good complement in fresh sweet corn.

. . . .

Melt the butter in a heavy soup pot over medium heat. When the butter froths and foams, stir in the chopped bacon, stirring as needed to prevent it from scorching, until it crisps and renders its fat, about 8 minutes.

Once the bacon crisps, use a slotted spoon to transfer it to a bowl, keeping as much of the rendered fat in the soup pot as you can. Turn down the heat beneath the pot to medium-low.

Stir the onion and celery into the hot fat, sautéing them together until they release their fragrance and soften, about 6 minutes. Dump the potatoes into the pot and pour the fish stock over them. Drop in the bay leaves and corn cobs. Turn down the heat to medium-low and simmer, covered, for 25 minutes, until the potatoes are tender.

Stir the corn kernels, jalapeño, and shrimp into the soup. Cover the pot once more and continue cooking until the corn is cooked through, about 10 minutes. Stir in the bacon and cream.

Ladle into soup bowls and serve warm.

seafood stew with lemony parsley pesto

serves 6

For the Seafood Stew

3 tablespoons olive oil

1 yellow onion, peeled and finely chopped

6 cloves garlic, minced

½ teaspoon crushed red pepper flakes

1 (14.5-ounce) can peeled and diced tomatoes, or 2 cups peeled, chopped fresh tomatoes

1 pound petite potatoes, peeled

½ cup dry white wine

2 cups Fish Stock (page 37)

2 bay leaves

¾ pound skinless black cod fillets

12 mussels, scrubbed and debearded

12 clams, scrubbed and debearded

1 pound spot shrimp, unpeeled

For the Parsley Pesto

2 cloves garlic, minced

1½ cups chopped fresh flat-leaf parsley

¼ cup pine nuts

2 tablespoons freshly grated lemon peel

½ cup extra-virgin olive oil

I love a hearty seafood stew. Dotted with fish, plenty of mussels, shrimp, and clams, this stew is brightened by the addition of lemon peel and fresh parsley. I like to serve this dish in early autumn when tomatoes are still ripe and plentiful but when the evening air takes a chill and my family wants something generous and warming. The key to this recipe is to leave the cod and shellfish to cook undisturbed, lest the cod flake apart as you stir it. You want to retain nice meaty chunks of fish for serving.

....

Make the seafood stew: Warm the olive oil in a Dutch oven over medium heat. When it releases its aroma, toss in the onion, garlic, and red pepper flakes, sautéing them in the hot oil until fragrant and translucent, about 8 minutes. Turn down the heat to medium-low and stir in the tomatoes, potatoes, wine, and fish stock. Drop in the bay leaves. Simmer, covered, until the potatoes yield when you pierce them with a fork, about 20 minutes.

Discard any clams and mussels that stay open when you tap on their shells. Remove the cover from the pot and place the cod fillets over the potatoes. Arrange the mussels, clams, and spot shrimp over the cod. Cover the pot once more and continue simmering the contents, undisturbed, until the fish flakes easily when pierced with a fork, the mussels and clams open, and the shrimp is cooked through, about 8 minutes further. Discard any mussels or clams that do not open.

Make the pesto: While the seafood cooks, toss the garlic, parsley, pine nuts, and lemon peel into the basin of a food processor and pulse twice to combine. Continue processing while pouring a thin stream of olive oil into the food processor. When all of the ingredients are combined into one uniform sauce, spoon it into a small bowl.

Ladle the warm soup into bowls and top with a dollop of the pesto.

salmon, celeriac, and potato chowder with dulse

serves 6

1 leek, root end and tough green parts reserved

2 sprigs thyme

2 bay leaves

2 teaspoons whole black peppercorns

2 tablespoons butter

1 teaspoon finely ground sea salt

½ teaspoon finely ground white pepper

1 small celeriac, chopped

¾ pound red potatoes, peeled and chopped

4 cups Sea Vegetable Broth (page 47)

¾ pound wild-caught skinless Alaskan salmon fillets, cut into 1-inch pieces

1 ounce dulse, picked over

1 cup heavy cream

A dark green, leafy seaweed with a briny and faintly sweet flavor, dulse makes a frequent appearance in traditional Irish cooking. Combined with salmon, cream, and potatoes, it creates a delicious chowder that's substantial enough to serve as a full meal. Dulse provides a dose of minerals and iodine, a nutrient that supports thyroid health. I favor using the Sea Vegetable Broth in this recipe, instead of a seafood based stock. Mild in flavor and utterly creamy, this chowder is a favorite on our dinner table, always served with a crusty loaf of whole-grain sourdough bread.

....

Tuck the root and leek greens into a 100% cotton muslin bag or tie them together in cheesecloth with the thyme, bay leaves, and black peppercorns.

Slice the white and light green part of the leek in half lengthwise and then slice it crosswise into half-moons about ¼ inch thick.

Warm the butter in a Dutch oven over medium heat. When the butter melts and begins to foam, stir in the sliced leek. Turn the heat down to medium-low and then sprinkle with the salt and white pepper. Cover the pot and let the leek sweat until fragrant and tender, about 8 minutes.

Stir the celeriac and potatoes into the softened leeks and then pour in the broth. Drop the sachet of herbs you prepared earlier in as well and then cover the pot and simmer for 20 minutes, or until the potatoes are barely tender.

Add the salmon and dulse and continue cooking, covered, for 10 minutes more, taking care not to disturb the pot as it cooks.

Turn off the heat and remove the sachet. Season to taste with sea salt, stir in the heavy cream, and serve warm.

why choose alaskan wild-caught salmon

Alaska's pristine waters provide a living for countless fishermen who catch wild salmon. These sustainably managed fisheries impose restrictions on salmon seasons, limiting catch and ensuring that wild salmon populations continue to proliferate. Alaska's thoughtful management of their waters and the fish that swim in them have become a model for sustainable fishing throughout the world.

Farmed salmon, by contrast, pose a risk to ocean ecology. Salmon farming concentrates fish, along with their waste, together within a confined space in the ocean. The buildup of waste encourages algae to bloom, which is then swept away and concentrated by oceanic currents into other areas, posing a threat to both farmed and wild fish. The more closely animals and fish are raised in proximity to one another, the easier it is for disease to spread, and to combat the inevitable spread of disease within fish farming systems, antibiotics are used within salmon aquaculture. Those antibiotics can then pass through the water's currents into the sea where they affect other fish, sea mammals, and organisms. Farmed salmon are also fed a manufactured feed, which is treated with dye to create a facsimile of the orange-pink color that wild salmon achieve through their diverse and natural diet. On top of all of this, open net systems used in salmon farming can ensnare marine seals, sea lions, and porpoises, resulting in the unnecessary deaths of marine mammals.

If you can, choose hook-and-line or troll-caught salmon, which are caught one at a time. In this traditional method of fishing, each salmon is handled with care, which reduces bruising that can impact the quality of the fish. For sources, see Where to Shop, page 172.

new england clam chowder

serves 6

1 tablespoon butter

2 ounces bacon, chopped into ¼-inch pieces

1 small yellow onion, peeled and chopped

4 celery stalks, chopped

1 pound waxy potatoes, peeled and chopped into ½-inch pieces

1 bay leaf

4 cups Fish Stock (page 37)

2 cups chopped cooked clams

1 teaspoon finely ground white pepper

2 teaspoons chopped fresh thyme

2 teaspoons chopped fresh flat-leaf parsley

2 cups heavy cream

Finely ground sea salt

I don't care for pasty chowders, gravy-like and thickened with flour, but I love the simplicity of New England clam chowder, touched by just enough cream to fortify the fish stock and coat soft and tender potatoes.

Among all the chowders I make at home, this version is my son's favorite—one that he asks for again and again and which I serve with homemade whole-grain rolls, straight out of the oven and buttered.

....

Warm the butter in a heavy soup pot over medium heat. When the butter begins to foam, stir in the bacon and let it render its fat and crisp, about 8 minutes. Once the bacon is nice and crisp, toss in the onion and celery, sautéing them in the hot fat until fragrant and translucent, about 6 minutes.

Stir in the potatoes, bay leaf, and fish stock and simmer them together, covered, until the potatoes yield when you pierce them with a fork, about 30 minutes.

Stir in the clams and cook until warmed through, about 4 minutes more. Stir in the white pepper, thyme, parsley, and cream.

Season to taste with a sprinkling of sea salt, ladle into soup bowls, and serve hot.

rhode island clear clam chowder

serves 6

2 bay leaves

3 sprigs thyme

1 tablespoon whole black peppercorns

1 tablespoon butter

8 ounces bacon, chopped into ¼-inch pieces

1 small onion, peeled and chopped

4 celery stalks, chopped

1 pound red potatoes, peeled and chopped

2 cups chopped cooked clams

6 cups Fish Stock (page 37)

My husband spent most of his childhood in Rhode Island, raised on the salty ocean air and seaside foods like fried clams, steamers, and chowder. During a visit to his hometown, we stopped at a clam shack near the beach where he introduced me to Rhode Island–style clam chowder. Unlike milky New England clam chowder or tomato-rich Manhattan clam chowder the Rhode Island variety, which is little more than a combination of clams, potatoes, and stock seasoned with bacon, is so plainly basic it's nearly austere, but in its plainness and simplicity, each of its ingredients shine.

....

Tuck the bay leaves, thyme, and peppercorns into a 100% cotton muslin bag or cheesecloth sachet and set it aside while you prepare the other ingredients.

Warm the butter in a soup pot over medium heat. When the butter begins to froth and foam, toss the bacon into the pot and fry it until it crisps in the hot fat, about 8 minutes.

Stir the onion and celery into the pot with the crisp bacon and sauté them together until they soften and release their fragrance, 6 minutes.

Stir the fish stock into the pot, bring it to a bare simmer, and then add the potatoes. Drop the sachet filled with herbs and peppercorns into the pot and simmer, covered, for 20 to 30 minutes, or until the potatoes are tender.

Stir the clams into the pot and cook them until they're warmed through but not rubbery, 4 minutes more.

Pluck the sachet of herbs out of the pot. Ladle the soup into soup bowls and serve hot.

thai-style spicy prawn soup
(tom yum goong)

serves 4

3 Thai chiles, smashed

1 (1-inch) knob ginger, peeled and sliced ⅛ inch thick

1 (6-inch) lemongrass stalk, tough outer layers removed, sliced ⅛ inch thick

3 makrut lime leaves

6 cups Shellfish Stock (page 40)

½ cup tomato puree

2 shallots, peeled and sliced paper thin

4 ounces mushrooms, preferably straw mushrooms, sliced ¼ inch thick or smaller

2 roma tomatoes, quartered

1 pound shelled prawns

2 tablespoons fish sauce

1 tablespoon palm sugar

Cilantro sprigs, for garnish

Thai basil leaves, for garnish

Lime wedges, for serving

Tom yum goong speaks loudly on the palate with fragrant notes of ginger, lemongrass, lime, and a potent punch of Thai chiles. It's a spicy Thai soup with pronounced sour notes balanced by a touch of sweetness. Its light and clear broth makes it a good starter. Many well-stocked supermarkets and natural foods stores will stock chiles, ginger, lemongrass, and lime leaves, but you might visit an Asian grocer to find both greater availability and more affordable prices.

....

Drop the chiles, ginger, lemongrass, and lime leaves into a soup pot and then cover them with the Shellfish Stock and tomato puree. Bring to a bare simmer over medium-high heat. Simmer, covered, for about 20 minutes, or until broth is fragrant.

Strain the stock into a pitcher or jar through a fine-mesh sieve, discarding the solids. Wipe out the soup pot with a kitchen towel to remove any stray debris.

Set the pot over medium-high heat and then pour the strained stock back into the pot. Toss in the shallots, mushrooms, tomatoes, and prawns and allow them to cook in the hot broth until the shrimp turns opaque and the mushrooms tender, about 8 minutes. Stir in the fish sauce and sugar, allowing it to cook until the sugar dissolves fully in the heat of the broth.

Ladle into soup bowls, and garnish with cilantro, Thai basil, and lime wedges.

simple miso soup with wakame

serves 4

4 cups Dashi (page 39)

2 tablespoons instant wakame flakes

2 tablespoons white miso paste

4 green onions

Simple Miso Soup is a beautiful blend of sweet, savory, and sour. It comes together in about the time it takes to boil a pot of water, making it nearly an instant soup. Many Japanese people begin their mornings simply with miso soup, rice, and pickled vegetables. Traditionally fermented miso is particularly rich in vitamin K and folate. To preserve its goodness, whisk the miso paste into the warm broth just before serving, as boiling it may damage its heat-sensitive nutrients.

....

Warm the dashi in a saucepan over medium-high heat until bubbles begin to form at the edges of the pan. Stir the wakame flakes into the broth, allowing them to rehydrate fully, about 2 minutes.

Turn off the heat, whisk in the miso paste until it dissolves fully, and then stir in the green onions.

Ladle into soup bowls and serve warm.

japanese hot pot with miso, clams, shiitakes, and leek (nabemono)

serves 4

4 cups Dashi (page 39)

¼ cup white miso

8 ounces winter or daikon radish, sliced ⅛ inch thick

8 ounces shiitakes, thinly sliced

1 leek, white and light green parts only, sliced

4 ounces spinach, stems removed, chopped coarsely

12 ounces clams, cleaned

2 tablespoons black sesame seeds

Wonderfully simple, nabemono is a traditional Japanese wintertime hot pot of simmering broth, vegetables, and seafood or meat. It all begins in a *nabe*, a squat, thick-walled, lidded pot typically made from earthenware or cast iron. You can often find *nabe* at reasonable prices in Asian grocers, but if you don't have one or don't have room for one in your kitchen, you can use a Dutch oven, a lidded braising dish, or a soup tureen.

This nabemono makes for a delightful presentation at the table, as you set the pot on a hot pad or trivet and lift the lid to release a plume of aromatic steam that dissipates to reveal beautifully colorful vegetables and just-opened clams. You can ladle the nabemono into individual bowls or, better yet, give your tablemates bowls, spoons, and chopsticks and allow them to pick and choose what they wish to add to their bowls.

....

Preheat the oven to 275°F.

Pour the dashi into a saucepan, cover it with a tight-fitting lid, and then bring it to a boil over medium-high heat.

While the dashi comes to a boil, prepare your *nabe*. Take a pastry brush and brush the miso paste along the inside of your pot in a thin, even coat, as though you were painting a canvas. Imagine your pot is split into four wedges. Each wedge will hold a single vegetable, as this makes it easier for your guests to pick and choose what they might add to their individual bowls. Arrange the radishes, mushrooms, leeks, and

continued

spinach evenly into the four quadrants of the *nabe*. Place the clams on top of the vegetables and then sprinkle the sesame seeds over them.

Pour the hot dashi over the clams and vegetables. Cover the *nabe* and transfer it to the oven. Bake for about 15 minutes, or until the clams open freely. Discard any clams that remain closed.

Remove the pot from the oven. You can spoon the vegetables and clams into individual bowls and ladle the broth over them or allow your guests to pick what they like from the pot, dropping it into their bowls and topping it off with a ladleful of broth.

vegetables

While bones bring protein to stocks and bone broths, vegetables and herbs bring minerals. These fragile foods release their minerals more readily than do bones. Vegetable broths can be assertive, with delightful green vegetal notes. While mineral-rich broths of kale, kombu, mushrooms, onion, and other vegetables can serve as a flavorful base for light vegetable soups, vegetables also partner beautifully with long-simmered stocks made from meaty bones, and their flavor is further enhanced by these robust stocks. You can pair them together for rich and satisfying soups, in risottos, or you can use stocks to braise vegetables, too, where their naturally occurring gelatin concentrates to produce a lovely glaze.

bieler's broth

serves 6

2 pounds zucchini, chopped

1 pound green beans, chopped into 1-inch pieces

2 celery stalks, chopped

1 bunch fresh parsley, plus more for garnish

Henry Bieler was a prominent twentieth-century physician who advocated for alternative medicine and treating disease with food. Among those foods he championed so fiercely was a broth made by simmering summer vegetables and parsley until softened and then pureeing them together. He felt this recipe would help detoxify and restore balance to the adrenal glands. Whether it performs any such function is debatable; however, it does make a lovely, light summer soup that is suitable for vegan diets. Season it well with salt, as its flavor is otherwise light and mild.

....

Drop all of the ingredients into a medium stockpot. Pour in enough water to cover by 1 inch and then bring it to a bare simmer over medium-high heat.

Turn down the heat to medium, and then simmer, covered, until the vegetables yield easily when pierced with a fork, about 15 minutes.

Using an immersion blender or food mill, puree the vegetables with their liquid. Season with salt, garnish with parsley and serve.

miso-glazed bok choy

serves 6

½ cup Dashi (page 39)

2 tablespoons white miso paste

1 teaspoon naturally fermented soy sauce

2 tablespoons toasted sesame oil

1 (1-inch) knob of ginger, sliced into matchsticks about 1 inch long

3 heads baby bok choy, halved lengthwise

2 tablespoons sesame seeds

When bok choy, a cruciferous vegetable with a pale, elongated stalk and broad, verdant leaves, first becomes available, usually in the early spring but often in autumn as well, I prefer dressing it simply and serving it on its own. In this recipe, it is paired with other subtle flavors, which complement rather than compete with its sweet and slightly peppery undertones

If you can, try to find baby bok choy for this dish. Not only is it less fibrous than large bok choy, but it also makes for a beautiful presentation.

. . . .

Warm the dashi in a small saucepan set over medium-low heat. When it's warm to the touch, turn off the heat and whisk in the miso paste and soy sauce until the miso fully dissolves and no clumps remain.

In a skillet with a tight-fitting lid, warm the sesame oil over medium heat. Toss the ginger into the hot oil, stirring it gently until it releases its sweet and spicy aroma. Add the bok choy halves, and fry cut side down in the ginger-infused oil, about 2 minutes. Turn them over and cook for 2 minutes more.

Pour the dashi mixture over the vegetables, turn down the heat to medium-low, and cover the skillet with a tight-fitting lid. Braise for 6 to 8 minutes, or until the bok choy is wilted.

Plate the cooked bok choy and any remaining juices and then sprinkle sesame seeds over the vegetables just before serving.

springtime risotto with asparagus, green garlic, and chive blossoms

serves 6

1 bunch fresh asparagus, peeled and chopped into ¼-inch lengths, stems and peels reserved

3 stems green garlic, white and light green parts peeled and finely chopped, dark green parts reserved

3 cups Whole Chicken Broth (page 28)

2 tablespoons extra-virgin olive oil

4 ounces prosciutto, sliced into ⅛ by 1-inch ribbons

2 cups carnaroli rice

1 cup dry white wine

¼ cup shredded Parmesan cheese

4 chive blossoms, or ¼ cup chopped fresh chives

Risotto is my go-to dinner when I'm feeling tired and worn out. It comes together relatively quickly, and the neutral flavor of both rice and broth gives risotto its versatility. I serve this dish in spring, when my garden and nearby farm stands brim with fresh asparagus, sharp green garlic, and purple-headed chive blossoms. Green garlic comes bunched together in long stems, like green onions, rather than in the bulbs that farmers harvest in late summer and autumn. You can usually find them, and chive blossoms, at a farmers' market or tucked into your CSA box if you don't happen to grow them yourself. If you can't find them, substitute a clove of garlic for each stem of green garlic.

....

Toss the woody asparagus stems and peelings and the dark green parts of the green garlic into a saucepan. Pour the broth into the pan and then set it over medium heat to warm.

Set a skillet or braising dish over medium heat and pour in the olive oil. When it's warm, stir in the prosciutto and chopped green garlic. Sauté them in the hot oil until they release their fragrance, about 4 minutes.

While the garlic and prosciutto cook, pour the rice into a fine-mesh sieve and rinse it in under running water until the water runs clear. Toss the rice into the pan with the garlic and prosciutto and then stir it continuously until the edges of the rice kernels turn translucent, about 5 minutes.

continued

Strain the broth through a fine-mesh sieve and into a heat-proof pitcher, discarding the vegetable trimmings. Ladle about ½ cup of broth into the rice and stir it continuously until the rice absorbs the liquid and then pour in another ½ cup. Continue stirring an additional ½ cup of broth into the rice every few minutes as the rice absorbs it until the rice is tender but not completely cooked through, 10 to 15 minutes.

Stir in the asparagus and then add the wine, stirring until the rice fully absorbs the liquid. Continue stirring until the rice is cooked through, 10 minutes more.

Stir in the Parmesan cheese so that it melts and mingles with the rice, then pluck the petals from the chive blossoms and scatter them over the rice.

Stir and serve warm.

roasted allium soup with fried leeks

serves 6

2 yellow onions, peeled, halved, and thinly sliced, peels reserved

3 shallots, peeled, halved, and thinly sliced, peels reserved

4 bulbs garlic, peeled and separated into cloves, peels reserved

2 tablespoons butter, melted

1 leek, white and light green thinly sliced, dark green parts reserved

4 cups Chicken Bone Broth (page 32)

6 sprigs thyme

¼ cup lard or olive oil

Finely ground sea salt

Sweet and savory at once, alliums are my favorite vegetable family. I love their sharpness when raw and the way that sharpness surrenders to heat, mellowing into a rich, complex sweetness.

I like to make this allium soup during the first few days of spring when the cool, wet chill in the air inevitably leaves me craving something both soothing and fortifying. In a single pot, I combine winter's last onions, shallots, and garlic together, topping them with spring's first leeks.

. . . .

Preheat the oven to 400°F.

Arrange the onions, shallots, and whole garlic cloves in a single layer on a baking sheet.

Drizzle the melted butter over the vegetables and bake them for 25 minutes, stirring once to promote even cooking.

Meanwhile, drop the reserved leek, onion, shallot, and garlic trimmings into a stockpot. Pour over the broth, drop in the thyme, cover the pot, and then bring it to a bare simmer over medium heat. Continue simmering for about 20 minutes, or until the broth smells fragrant. Strain through a fine-mesh sieve into a heat-proof jar or pitcher and discard the solids.

Remove the baking sheet from the oven and spoon the roasted vegetables into the now-empty stockpot. Pour in the flavored broth and bring to a bare simmer over medium heat. Simmer the soup, covered, for 20 minutes, tasting it to make sure the flavors of the vegetables have blended well.

continued

Line a plate with a paper towel or kitchen linen. While the soup simmers, warm the lard over medium-high heat until it begins to shimmer. Working with about ¼ cup at a time, spoon the sliced leeks into the hot fat, taking care to avoid splattering. Fry the leeks until golden and crisp, about 8 minutes. Using a slotted spoon, transfer the leeks to the lined plate to allow any residual cooking fat to drain away.

Turn off the heat beneath the soup and then puree the soup with an immersion blender or food mill until creamy and uniformly smooth.

Season to taste with sea salt, ladle it into soup bowls, and sprinkle with the fried leeks just before serving.

fresh pea soup with spring herbs

serves 6

3½ pounds fresh English peas, shelled, or 4 cups frozen shelled peas

3 tablespoons butter

1 leek, white and light green parts only, thinly sliced

½ teaspoon finely ground sea salt

4 cups Green Broth (page 43)

¼ cup chopped fresh flat-leaf parsley

¼ cup chopped fresh mint, plus more for garnish

¼ cup chopped fresh chives

1 cup heavy cream

In May, when all things green seem to spring exuberantly from the ground, the weekly box that we pick up from a nearby farm brims with plump English peas, ready to shell. My son happens to love the painstaking chore of shelling peas. He likes to crush the pod lightly between his thumb and forefinger, until it opens at the seam, and then he flicks the peas into the bowl. Pea season lasts only a few weeks, after which the weather is too hot for them to continue to produce. Beautifully, though, their season coincides with the first bunch of green herbs that begin to appear at market: mint, chives, and parsley. These ingredients belong together.

....

If you're working with fresh shelled peas, drop them into a large mixing bowl. Discard any mushy pods or yellowed peas. If you're working with frozen peas, set them out on the countertop to thaw.

Warm the butter in a soup pot over medium-low heat. Once it has melted, turn the heat up to medium and drop in the sliced leeks. Sprinkle them with the salt and cover the pot, allowing them to sweat until softened and tender, about 10 minutes.

Toss the peas into the pot, pour in the broth, and simmer, covered, until the peas are soft and tender yet still bright green. If you're working with fresh peas, allow 20 to 25 minutes for them to cook through. Frozen peas, already cooked, need only 5 to 8 minutes to heat through.

Turn off the heat, stir in the herbs, and then puree the soup with an immersion blender or in a blender, filling the blender no more than half full with each batch of soup until smooth.

Stir in the cream, season to taste with sea salt, and ladle into soup bowls. Garnish with chopped mint and serve warm.

roasted mushrooms with rye berries

Serves 4

2 cups rye berries, picked over

1 tablespoon apple cider vinegar

1 pound mushrooms, stems reserved, caps sliced ⅛ inch thick

4 cups Roasted Mushroom Broth (page 44)

2 tablespoons butter

2 shallots, peeled and thinly sliced

3 celery stalks, thinly sliced

Finely ground sea salt

1 tablespoon fresh thyme leaves

In early autumn, my son and I head to the forest and collect mushrooms together. Over the years, he has developed a keen eye for spotting young golden chanterelles nestled in pockets of pine needles. I favor robust, cinnamon-capped porcini mushrooms, though, in earnest, we forage those edibles we can find and are glad for them. When roasted, mushrooms develop a robust meaty flavor, which pairs well with whole grains and rye berries in particular. Lovely on its own, you can also serve this dish alongside roasted turkey or beef. Any mushrooms will work in this recipe, wild or cultivated, but aim for a variety for best results.

....

In a mixing bowl, add the rye berries and then pour in enough warm water to cover by 2 inches. Stir in the vinegar and allow the rye berries to soak for at least 12 and up to 24 hours. Drain them through a fine-mesh sieve and then rinse well, returning the soaked berries to the mixing bowl.

Drop the mushroom stems into a saucepan, pour in the broth, and simmer them together over medium heat. Allow the stems to simmer in the broth while you prepare the other ingredients, or about ten minutes—long enough for the mushrooms to release their flavor.

Warm the butter in a wide skillet over medium-high heat. When it melts and begins to froth, stir in the shallots and celery, sautéing until fragrant and translucent. Stir in the mushroom caps and sauté for another 5 minutes. Stir in the rye berries and cook for 4 minutes more.

Strain the broth, discarding the solids, and stir it into the soaked rye berries ½ cup at a time, making sure that the berries fully absorb the broth before adding more. Continue stirring the broth into the rye berries, until the rye berries are tender.

Season with salt, sprinkle with fresh thyme, and serve warm.

roasted beet soup with dill and horseradish sour cream

serves 6

2 pounds red beets

6 cups Long-Simmered Roasted Beef Bone Broth (page 34)

1 teaspoon whole black peppercorns

1 bay leaf

2 tablespoons butter

2 shallots, peeled and minced

1 celery stalk, finely chopped

Finely ground sea salt and freshly ground black pepper

½ cup sour cream

2 tablespoons freshly grated horseradish

2 tablespoons minced fresh dill

With its fleeting yet flavorful heat, horseradish brings balance to the rich sweetness of roasted beets in this simple and cleansing soup. Despite the inclusion of beef broth, hearty beets, and sour cream, this is a light soup, and one that pairs well with a slice of toasted sourdough bread spread thickly with chicken liver pâté.

....

Preheat the oven to 400°F.

Wrap the beets in parchment paper and set them on a baking sheet in the oven. Roast them for 45 minutes, until deeply fragrant and soft enough that you can pierce them with a knife, meeting no resistance at their center.

While the beets roast, pour the broth into a soup pot and drop in the peppercorns and bay leaf. Cover the pot and keep the broth warm over medium-low heat while it infuses with the flavor of the peppercorns and bay.

Remove the beets from the oven and let them cool until they're comfortable enough to handle. Slip off their skins and chop them into ½-inch pieces.

Strain the broth through a fine-mesh sieve into a heat-proof jar or pitcher, discarding the peppercorns and bay leaf. Wipe the soup pot clean with a kitchen towel and then melt the butter in the pot over medium-high heat. Toss in the shallots and the celery and sauté them in the hot butter until fragrant and softened, about 8 minutes.

Add the broth, stir in the roasted beets, and simmer for 10 minutes, just long enough to warm the beets through and allow their bright pigments to color the soup. Season to taste with salt and pepper.

Whisk the horseradish into the sour cream. Ladle the soup into bowls and top with a dollop of horseradish sour cream and a sprinkling of fresh dill.

irish vegetable soup

serves about 6

3 carrots, peeled and chopped into ½-inch pieces

2 parsnips, peeled and chopped into ½-inch pieces

1 celeriac, peeled and chopped into ½-inch pieces

2 potatoes, peeled and chopped into ½-inch pieces

3 tablespoons butter

1 leek, white and light green parts, thinly sliced

1 teaspoon fresh thyme leaves, plus more for garnish

½ teaspoon finely ground sea salt

4 cups Long-Simmered Roasted Pork Bone Broth (page 38)

1 cup heavy cream

Crème fraîche, for serving (optional)

I visited Ireland for the first time when I was nineteen. With little pocket money to keep me fed, I relied on inexpensive bowls of sweet and earthy pureed vegetable soup. Soup like this was served nearly everywhere and always with a hunk of brown soda bread spread thickly with butter. If you can't find parsnips, substitute with rutabaga, another root vegetable beloved in traditional Irish cooking.

Dump the carrots, parsnips, celeriac, and potatoes into a large mixing bowl and set aside.

Melt the butter in a heavy soup pot over medium heat. When it froths and foams, add the leeks and sprinkle with the thyme and salt. Cover the pot with a tight-fitting lid, allowing the leeks to sweat in the pot with butter and thyme until they soften, about 10 minutes.

Uncover the pot, stir in the chopped vegetables, and then pour the broth over them. Return the cover to the pot and turn down the heat to medium-low. Allow the vegetables to simmer together in the pot until fork-tender, about 30 minutes.

Turn off the heat. Puree the soup with an immersion blender or food mill until smooth and uniform. Stir in the fresh cream, ladle into soup bowls, and serve warm. If it suits you, spoon a dollop of crème fraîche into your bowl and garnish with fresh thyme.

carrot and leek soup with thyme

serves 6

1 tablespoon butter

1 leek, white and light green parts only, thinly sliced

1 teaspoon finely ground sea salt

1 pound carrots, peeled and sliced ¼ inch thick

2 teaspoons fresh thyme leaves, plus more for garnish

4 cups Sea Vegetable Broth (page 47)

Finely ground sea salt

1 cup crème fraîche

There's a farm five miles down the road from our home known for its impossibly large, juicy, and candy-sweet carrots. The sweetness of carrots can easily overpower other foods, so they need to be tempered by other pronounced but complementary flavors: I favor fresh thyme with its sharp herbal notes, which introduces a savory aspect to this carrot soup. Crème fraîche, nearly always a good addition to swirl into the soup pot at the end of cooking, adds both richness and a light, tart flavor that nicely rounds out this dish.

....

Melt the butter in a heavy soup pot over medium-low heat. Drop the leeks into the melted butter and sprinkle them with the salt. Cover the pot and let the leeks sweat until softened, about 8 minutes.

Drop the carrots and thyme into the leeks, pour in the broth, and simmer, covered, until the carrots fall apart easily when you pierce them with a fork, about 25 minutes.

Puree the soup with an immersion blender or in batches in a blender and then season with sea salt.

Stir in the crème fraîche, ladle into soup bowls, garnish with thyme, and serve warm.

roasted tomato and fennel soup

serves 6

2 pounds Roma or Striped Roman tomatoes, peeled and cut in half lengthwise

1 yellow onion, peeled, halved, and thinly sliced

1 fennel bulb, quartered, stemmed, and cored; chopped into ½-inch pieces; fronds reserved

1 tablespoon olive oil

4 cups Long-Simmered Roasted Pork Broth (page 36)

Finely ground sea salt

Sour cream or crème fraîche, for serving

There's a brief period of time, a few weeks only, when the seasons for tomatoes and fennel overlap. Fennel, typically preferring cooler weather, fades out in late July, while tomatoes are only just coming into their prime. Pairing them together makes a rich orange-red soup with the bright, acidic flavors of tomatoes at the forefront and the subtle, fleeting, anise-like sweetness of fennel as a top note. A meaty tomato variety like Roma will give your soup a nice thickness. If you can find them, Striped Roman tomatoes, a beautiful heirloom variety with an egg-like shape and a brilliant red-orange color striated with yellow, are a nice choice, too.

....

Preheat the oven to 425°F.

Arrange the tomatoes, cut side up, on a baking sheet. Sprinkle the onion slices and fennel pieces over the tomatoes and then drizzle with olive oil.

Set baking sheet in the oven to roast for 20 minutes, stirring once to ensure even cooking.

Spoon the roasted vegetables into a soup pot and then pour in the broth. Simmer, covered, over medium-high heat until the flavors are well blended, about 20 minutes.

While the soup simmers, chop the reserved fennel fronds.

Puree the soup with an immersion blender or food mill and then salt the soup as you like it.

Ladle into soup bowls, spoon a dollop of sour cream over the soup, and sprinkle each serving with reserved chopped fennel fronds.

tallow-roasted onions with fresh rosemary

serves 6

¼ cup Long-Simmered Roasted Beef Bone Broth (page 34) plus ¼ cup reserved beef tallow

6 yellow onions, stems and roots trimmed, skins intact

2 teaspoons coarsely ground sea salt

1 teaspoon coarsely ground black pepper

3 sprigs rosemary

In December, when our CSA closes for the season, I visit our farmer to pick up our last box of fresh vegetables. I usually order a few additional boxes of root vegetables, winter squash, garlic, and onions to help us ride out the dark days until spring in all its plenty arrives again. Among the many dishes we make with our bounty is roasted onions. Roasting softens an onion's assertiveness, reducing it to a mellow sweetness and delicate tenderness. Fresh rosemary with its bright herbal perfume complements this sweetness and provides a touch of savory, too. I like to serve these onions alongside roast beef or roast leg of lamb.

....

Preheat the oven to 400°F.

Pour the broth into a small saucepan and warm it over low heat until any gelatin present melts back into a liquid.

Arrange the onions in a baking dish and then top each one with a dollop of tallow, about 2 teaspoons for each. Sprinkle the onions with salt and pepper. Gently pull off the needles from each sprig of rosemary and sprinkle them evenly over each onion. Pour the warm broth around the onions and into the bottom of the baking dish and bake in the hot oven until the onions are tender, about 40 minutes.

Remove the onions from the oven, allowing them to cool slightly. Gently pull off and discard each onion skin and then serve the onions warm.

potato and onion gratin

serves 6

2 tablespoons butter

2 pounds Yukon gold potatoes, peeled and sliced ⅛ inch thick

2 yellow onions, peeled, halved, and sliced ⅛ inch thick

2 tablespoons fresh thyme leaves

1 cup Long-Simmered Roasted Beef Bone Broth (page 34)

1 cup heavy cream

1 teaspoon finely ground sea salt

2 ounces Gruyère cheese

Onions soften and sweeten with prolonged cooking, the heat of a bubbling pot or the oven melting away their raw, assertive sharpness. In this gratin, they bake with potatoes in cream and broth seasoned with salt and fresh thyme until impossibly tender. While it's relatively laborious to slice potatoes and onions thin enough for a gratin, doing so yields lovely results, and I like to save this dish for company. Uniformity is key in making potato gratin, as the cooking times of potatoes and onions sliced in varying thicknesses will differ. You can slice them by hand, or use a mandolin to give you uniformly thin rounds of potatoes and onion.

....

Butter a 2-quart baking dish and preheat the oven to 375°F.

Carefully arrange half of the potatoes in a single layer of overlapping slices at the bottom of the buttered dish. Arrange the onions in overlapping slices in a single layer on top of the potatoes and then sprinkle them with half of the thyme leaves. Cover the onions and thyme with a second layer of potatoes.

Pour the broth and cream into a small mixing bowl or pitcher and then whisk in the salt. Pour the seasoned broth and cream over the layers of potatoes and onions, and then sprinkle the top of the potatoes with the remaining thyme leaves.

Using a fine grater or a Microplane, shred the cheese evenly over the top of the potatoes.

Bake the gratin until the potatoes are very tender, yielding easily when pierced with a fork, and the liquid is mostly absorbed, about 1 hour.

Remove from the oven, allowing the gratin to cool for about 5 minutes, and then serve warm, directly from the pan.

where to shop

Visit a nearby farmers' market, farm stand, or natural foods market to find a local source for bones and meat to make your broth, as well as ingredients to make the soups, stews, and other dishes found within this book. If you have trouble finding sources locally, consider buying from any of the providers below, each of whom specializes in nutrient-dense whole foods.

. . . .

for meat and bones for your broth

Eat Wild
www.eatwild.com

Provides listings of farms that produce grass-fed beef and lamb as well as pasture-raised pork and chicken.

Tendergrass Farms
www.tendergrass.com

Provides grass-fed beef, pasture-raised pork, and pasture-raised chicken, including bones for broth and stock making.

for wild-caught fish and shellfish

Alaska Gold Brand by the Seafood Producers Cooperative
www.alaskagoldbrand.com

The fishermen-owned Seafood Producers Cooperative provides wild Alaskan salmon, black cod, albacore tuna, and halibut, all caught one fish at a time by hook and line.

Vital Choice
www.vitalchoice.com

Provider of wild-caught fish and sustainable seafood like Alaskan cod, clams, mussels, oysters, spot shrimp, and Oregon pink shrimp.

for wholesome fats

Pure Indian Foods
www.pureindianfoods.com

Maker of grass-fed, organic ghee as well as cold-pressed sesame oil.

Jovial Foods
www.jovialfoods.com

Maker of organic extra-virgin olive oil from heirloom olive varieties.

Chaffin Family Orchards
 www.chaffinfamilyorchards.com

Third-generation biodiverse California family farm that sells olive oil.

Fatworks Foods
www.fatworks.com

Maker of tallow from grass-fed beef, lard from pasture-raised pigs, as well as rendered duck fat from free-range ducks.

for prepared stocks, broths, and bone broths

The Brothery
www.bonebroth.com

Maker of chicken and beef bone broth simmered with aromatic vegetables, ginger, lemon, and herbs.

Wise Choice Market
www.wisechoicemarket.com

Provides chicken and beef bone broth simmered with aromatic vegetables and fresh herbs, as well as fish stock.

bibliography

Allen, Ann. *The Housekeepers' Assistant.* J. Munroe, 1845.

Beecher, Esther. *Miss Beecher's Domestic Receipt Book.* Harper, 1850.

Beull Hale, Sarah. *The Good Housekeeper.*
Weeks, Jordan and Company, 1839.

Croly, Jane. *Jennie June's Book of American Cookery.*
The American News Co., 1870.

Ladies of the First Presbyterian Church. Oliver Crook, 1873.
The First Presbyterian Church Cookbook.

Molokhovets, Elena. *Classic Russian Cooking: A Gift to Young Housewives.*
Trans. Joyce Toomre. Indiana University Press, 1998.

Newton Foote Henderson, Mary. *Practical Cooking and Dinner Giving.*
Harper & Brothers, 1877.

Price, Weston, DDS. *Nutrition and Physical Degeneration.* 8th ed.
Price Pottenger Nutrition, 2009.

measurement conversion charts

Volume

us	imperial	metric
1 tablespoon	½ fl oz	15 ml
2 tablespoons	1 fl oz	30 ml
¼ cup	2 fl oz	60 ml
⅓ cup	3 fl oz	90 ml
½ cup	4 fl oz	120 ml
⅔ cup	5 fl oz (¼ pint)	150 ml
¾ cup	6 fl oz	180 ml
1 cup	8 fl oz (⅓ pint)	240 ml
1¼ cups	10 fl oz (½ pint)	300 ml
2 cups (1 pint)	16 fl oz (⅔ pint)	480 ml
2½ cups	20 fl oz (1 pint)	600 ml
1 quart	32 fl oz (1⅔ pints)	1 l

Temperature

fahrenheit	celsius/gas mark
250°F	120°C/gas mark ½
275°F	135°C/gas mark 1
300°F	150°C/gas mark 2
325°F	160°C/gas mark 3
350°F	175 or 180°C/gas mark 4
375°F	190°C/gas mark 5
400°F	200°C/gas mark 6
425°F	220°C/gas mark 7
450°F	230°C/gas mark 8
475°F	245°C/gas mark 9
500°F	260°C

Length

inch	metric
¼ inch	6 mm
½ inch	1.25 cm
¾ inch	2 cm
1 inch	2.5 cm
6 inches (½ foot)	15 cm
12 inches (1 foot)	30 cm

Weight

us/imperial	metric
½ oz	15 g
1 oz	30 g
2 oz	60 g
¼ lb	115 g
⅓ lb	150 g
½ lb	225 g
¾ lb	350 g
1 lb	450 g

gratitude

Thank you to my husband and son who withstood long nights, broth-making marathons, and taste-testing soups, stocks, and stews every night for three months straight. I love you both so very much. Thank you to Sally Ekus for always being an advocate. Thank you to the team at Ten Speed Press for their unwavering patience and insight. Thank you to the many steadfast readers of Nourished Kitchen for their many years of support.

index

Published in the United States by Ten Speed Press,
an imprint of the Crown Publishing Group, a division
of Penguin Random House LLC, New York.
www.crownpublishing.com
www.tenspeed.com

Ten Speed Press and the Ten Speed Press colophon are
registered trademarks of Penguin Random House LLC.

Library of Congress Cataloging-in-Publication Data
Names: McGruther, Jennifer, author.
Title: Broth and stock from the Nourished kitchen : wholesome
    master recipes and how to cook with them / by Jennifer McGruther.
Description: First edition. | Berkeley : Ten Speed Press, 2016. | Includes
    bibliographical references and index.
Identifiers: LCCN 2015036644
Subjects: LCSH: Soups. | Stews. | BISAC: COOKING / Specific Ingredients /
    Natural Foods. | COOKING / Courses & Dishes / Soups & Stews. | COOKING /
    Health & Healing / General. | LCGFT: Cookbooks.
Classification: LCC TX757 .M427 2016 | DDC 641.81/3--dc23

Trade Paperback ISBN: 978-1-60774-931-8
eBook ISBN: 978-1-60774-932-5

Printed in China

Design by Nami Kurita

10 9 8 7 6 5 4 3 2 1

First Edition